# NEW HOME COOKING

# NEW HOME COOKING
## FEEDING FAMILY, FEASTING FRIENDS

◆

## FLORENCE FABRICANT

Photographs by John Dugdale

**Clarkson Potter/Publishers**
**New York**

# *To Richard, Patty, and Robert*
# *with love*

*Copyright © 1991 by Florence Fabricant*

*Published by Clarkson N. Potter, Inc.,
201 East 50th Street, New York, New York 10022.
Member of the Crown Publishing Group.
CLARKSON N. POTTER, POTTER, and colophon are trademarks of
Clarkson N. Potter, Inc.*

*Manufactured in Japan*

*Designed by Brenda Wolf*

*Library of Congress Cataloging-in-Publication Data
Fabricant, Florence.
New home cooking: Feeding family, feasting friends/by Florence Fabricant.——1st ed.
p.   cm.
Includes index.
1. Cookery.   2. Menus.   I. Title.
TX714.F33   1991*

*641.5——dc20*                                                    *90-47218*

*CIP
ISBN 0-517-57722-4*

*1   3   5   7   9   10   8   6   4   2*

*First Edition*

# ACKNOWLEDGMENTS

My career as a food writer and cookbook author has not been shaped by one mentor: many colleagues as well as giants in the field have influenced my work. I am deeply grateful to Craig Claiborne and Julia Child. Their accomplishments have always been an inspiration; their generous words of praise never cease to stun me. I am also indebted to Paula Wolfert, David Liederman, Gael Greene, Sheila Lukins, Julee Rosso, Pierre Franey, Niki Singer, Elizabeth Schneider, Lorenza de'Medici, Joyce Goldstein, Rozanne Gold, Raymond Sokolov, Miles and Lillian Cahn, Susy Davidson, Marian Burros, Molly O'Neill, Horace Sutton, Sam Aaron, Roger Yaseen, Julie Sahni, Eric Asimov, Angela Dodson, and Ken Hom for their encouragement, their exacting standards, and their wonderfully enriching friendship.

My thanks also go to many readers of my columns and articles who have taken time to write letters of appreciation for recipes that work, and to many friends and colleagues who have shown their approval by cleaning their plates and asking for seconds at my table.

This project depended on a number of talents other than my own: Pam Krauss's canny yet graceful editing, John Dugdale's luminous photography, Bruce Cliborne and Rosco Betsill's cooking and styling done with flair and sensitivity, and Brenda Wolf's elegant design. Billy and Tom of Pure Madderlake and Valerie Hart of Valerie Hart designs lent both their homes and lovely flowers for photography. Thanks, too, to Terry Mulligan, who was always ready to retype. And, of course, it could not have happened without my energetic agent, Jane Dystel.

# CONTENTS

# FOREWORD

Our friendship with Florence goes back many years, and over that time she has played a very enriching role in our lives. Her passionate curiosity about and vast knowledge of food, style, and entertaining have been an ongoing inspiration. From the very first page of *New Home Cooking* you feel Florence welcoming you at her door and drawing you into her family circle filled with caring and warmth. Luscious smells from Plum and Oat-Bran Betty to Coq au Vin with Shiitake Mushrooms waft from within.

A personal sense of her own traditions and comforting remembrances of the family kitchen in which she grew up are apparent throughout. It was with great pleasure that she watched her mother preparing potato pasta and other wonderful dishes from only the freshest ingredients, knowing that she always set a gracious table both for family and friends. This is the honest, yet eclectic style that so many of us are longing to recapture.

We are thrilled with the overflowing market basket of carefully chosen ingredients used in each menu and recipe. Their wealth ranges from succulent black and purple figs, fresh asparagus, ripe Italian prune plums, and fresh rhubarb to rabbit, mako shark, pearly scallops, and the perfect chicken. Yet we never feel limited to or intimidated by the vaguely unfamiliar or exotic. Pot roast, mashed potatoes, Cherry Tomato Compote, and Old-fashioned Chocolate Pudding weave easily together with Pappa al Pomodoro, Caesared Green Bean Salad, Lemon-Pepper Pears Splashed with Grappa, and Deep Chocolate Chunk Loaf.

Cooking with Florence is often reminiscent of unforgettable vacations. She takes us on "The Grand Tour," blending cultures with classical preparations. Flavors from the Far East are as accessible as those of the Southwest. Eastern European dishes warm the body and soul as the best of Tuscany never ceases to delight. With great intelligence and good sense, Florence has brought all these riches home.

For those who find organization and menu planning totally elusive, she shows us how. There is never a need to press the panic button. Once your kitchen is established, cooking on a regular basis becomes an integral part of a relaxed, ongoing life-style. Meals can be prepared on the spur of the moment with the right ingredients always on hand. Leftovers from one meal can be deliciously transformed into another. Seasonal cravings are the icing on the cake—special for both family and friends.

Most importantly, Florence shares with us her own personal life-style. Her family meals, often prepared ensemble, are always special, even if the fare is homey and simple. When friends gather, the same gracious ease is displayed, making everyone feel very much a part of her extended family.

We love this book and feel that all its many aspects encourage us to take the time to achieve a great quality of life. *The New Home Cooking* is a personal adventure and always cleverly creative. Thank you, Florence, for sharing your own style with us.

—*Sheila Lukins and Julee Rosso*

# INTRODUCTION

When it comes to style, there's nothing like homestyle. It puts guests, whether friends or relatives, at ease while it makes cooking and serving delightfully relaxed for the host or hostess. It's the way I entertain and the way I cook on a daily basis.

Today, few people have time to devote to good cooking. I've found when friends are invited for dinner, they most enjoy being served slowly simmered stews like my coq au vin because it's the type of dish they rarely bother with at home for themselves. And while I might add stylish touches to the garnish or an extra course or two to the menu plan, I would not hesitate to anchor a Saturday night dinner party with big bowls of hearty borscht in winter, or a substantial salad of seasonal offerings in summer.

Painstaking garnishes, breathtaking arrangements, and astonishingly costly out-of-season ingredients have never been my style. These elements are not what make an evening special. Rather, the criteria, when entertaining as well as when serving the family, should be taste, eye appeal, and satisfaction. My menus are designed with the goals of creating a balance of ingredients and dishes that makes for a harmonious ensemble.

I love it when others at the table—friends or family—can't resist a second helping or find the food overcomes their willpower. And while I do not serve huge portions or attempt to undermine diets, I do believe wonderful-tasting food to be one of life's great rewards.

For many Americans, home cooking as we knew it before and after World War II and until the late 1970s hardly exists anymore. Dinner has somehow become an afterthought, necessary to assuage hunger but best accomplished in the least amount of time. Menus based on processed convenience foods or a quick dash to a restaurant are increasingly the norm.

But there is a backlash.

Young people who grew up in families where little or no real cooking was done yearn to understand and to taste lovingly prepared, delicious food. They are willing to learn what their mothers, working women too tired to cook, did not teach them. It is a heartening development, one that I readily endorse.

But by the same token, few of us are interested in spending days crafting elaborate dinner parties composed of restaurant-style food, the way we did ten or fifteen years ago. The food that appeals to us now, both for family meals and to share with company, is unpretentious, inviting fare full of flavor and naturally eye-appealing.

Even restaurants are now finding that dishes such as mashed potatoes and homey stews are becoming their best-sellers. The resurgence of bistro fare attests to our preference for simple, satisfying, reassuring food. Dishes such as rice and beans or bread pudding, once scorned as "peasant food," now bring raves for the home cook and professional chef alike.

I feel fortunate—blessed, in fact—that my mother was a superb cook and that I was raised in a family that loved good food. So many of my contemporaries, my husband included, can only recall how their mothers spent all day cooking—the green beans.

My mother cared about using ingredients of the best quality, and she treated them with respect. She enjoyed entertaining and preparing foods from scratch in an era when adding a can of soup was the accepted way to make a fancy cream sauce. The milk bottle never went directly on the table; its contents were transferred to a pitcher, even when she was pressed for time. Some of her recipes and more of her sound notions about how to craft a satisfying meal have shaped the way I cook and serve and are incorporated into this book.

Hers are the chicken in the pot with limpid, golden flavorful soup and "pasta" made with mashed potatoes in the dough, an Eastern European dish expressed in contemporary terms. It was the cooking she learned from her mother, who taught her, as she taught me, that you cannot rush the sautéed onions and expect to achieve proper results, and that you must taste for seasoning and rely on your judgment instead of merely depending on formulas.

This is the way I cook and the way my children have learned to cook. It is the way I would encourage my readers to cook, using my menus and recipes as a foundation for their own tastes and ideas. It is what makes good home-cooked food possible on a daily basis because, at its foundation, homestyle cooking (and entertaining) depends most of all on sound basics: the satisfaction that comes from a pasta boiled and sauced just so, impeccably fresh fish perfectly sizzled on the grill, a loaf of honest, crusty wheat bread, a succulently ripe tomato simply dressed with fragrant olive oil and a splash of rich wine vinegar. It's an attitude toward food and cooking that I know the friends and family who gather at your table will respond to as warmly as those at my table have.

## ENTERTAINING AT HOME: THE TIME FACTOR

How fast can a meal be prepared? Once the standard for speed was an hour, then it was thirty minutes, then twenty. Yet in some ways, these times are deceptive; it may take no longer to put together a savory, long-simmered soup or stew than to prepare a grilled chicken breast, because the stew cooks virtually by itself, and the satisfaction derived from the former, as well as the supply of welcome leftovers, can be so much greater. Some days might offer the hours I need to prepare a succulent pot roast or fresh loaves of bread, and at other times my schedule demands a quick scallopini or bowl of pasta topped with uncooked chopped tomatoes. Most important, my guests are content with either menu.

Still, few of us have unlimited amounts of time to spend in the kitchen. I am an efficient cook and I find I can reduce the time it takes to prepare a dinner by careful planning. A number of the menus in this book require no more than thirty minutes to assemble. In the introductions to the various menus I indicate the order in which the dishes should be prepared to accomplish the cooking most expediently. Efficiency in the kitchen also depends on careful planning and on feeling comfortable with a variety of basic kitchen techniques. The more you cook, the better and easier the cooking becomes.

Time-saving appliances are a boon. I rely on my food processor for many tasks, often planning the order in which I process foods so that the machine does not require washing in between. My electric mixer facilitates baking jobs so that cakes needn't be made only for special occasions. An electric coffee grinder guarantees a delicious finale for the meal.

Though I do use a microwave oven, I do not depend on it for cooking. It is indispensable for reheating, for accelerating thawing, and for some basic preparations such as producing the equivalent of steamed vegetables in a trice. But just as I still enjoy kneading bread by hand instead of using my electric mixer's dough hook—to me there is no substitute for the feel of properly kneaded dough (to say nothing of the exercise)—I also like being able to tend my food, watching how a roasting chicken or a stew or a soup is doing and making necessary adjustments as I go. I use all five senses when I cook.

Rather than rely on the speed of microwave cooking, I concentrate on careful planning. A potato bakes in forty-five minutes to an hour from the time the conventional oven is lit. Rarely must I walk in the door and have dinner ready to eat in less time than that. And if I must, I replace baked potatoes (which, incidentally, are never as delicious when cooked in a microwave oven) in the menu with boiled potatoes or rice, ready in twenty minutes—or pasta, which cooks in less than ten minutes, or couscous, which needs a mere five.

In general, I find that as long as my knives are sharp, it's the marketing that demands more time than the actual preparation of the meal. But smart shopping can also save time. Knowing where to buy excellent bread, picking up a barbecued chicken at a food shop to use for a last-minute chicken salad or the main dish for a light lunch, buying commercially prepared stuffed vine leaves or ordering some Chinese dumplings from a restaurant to serve as appetizers are all excellent ploys that do not diminish the overall quality of a meal.

When I am entertaining or preparing a dinner for more than four, however, I try to plan menus to avoid searching for esoteric or out-of-season ingredients. Keeping the calendar and market availability in mind when planning menus is one way to make preparation faster and more convenient. Having a well-stocked larder is another.

## SELECTING INGREDIENTS

Today's kitchen is open to the cuisines of the world: the heat of hot peppers, the exotic pungency of fresh coriander, and the bright crunch of snow peas. Varying the menu, adding a personal touch to the seasonings, and exploring culinary frontiers have become easier than ever. For example, my children's repertory, like mine, is far more diverse than those of earlier generations. The recipes they have contributed to this book include vegetarian couscous and a beef salad spiced with chilies and fortified with beans—foods of the sort they have sampled in restaurants and in their travels. Their tastes include many Asian and Middle Eastern cuisines, as well as the cooking of Italy, France, Spain, and Mexico.

The international market basket is now a convenient one to fill. Purchasing soy sauce, extra-virgin olive oil, French cornichons, or bulghur wheat no longer involves a trip to a specialty store. These and hundreds of other foods are now among the 25,000 or more items routinely stocked in supermarkets.

In addition, demand for the likes of fresh ginger, radicchio, goat cheeses, and even caviar has given rise to domestic producers, so it is no longer necessary to rely on imports. Ingredients once limited to regional cooks, such as fresh chilies and catfish, are now sold across the country. And delicacies that were once ignored—chanterelle mushrooms and monkfish, for example—are available and in demand.

Cooking today has been shaped by recent agricultural and commercial developments, from the year-round availability of once-seasonal items such as fresh herbs to the widespread marketing of balsamic vinegar for the green salad. Ingredients used in restaurants are now sold in retail markets, and recipes by chefs fill the pages of newspapers, magazines, and books. And if we think we have seen it all, we are in for a surprise, as new dietary information is announced, changing our notion of a well-balanced meal. Environmental concerns have become more compelling, also affecting what we eat.

When I see something new or unusual while shopping—an odd-looking melon, an unfamiliar variety of fish, or dried beans in an unlikely color—I'm quick to buy it, take it home, and try it. While it makes sense to avoid fads, shopping and cooking with a little daring and adventure is exciting.

Still, the primary consideration when filling a shopping cart is quality. A dish is only as good as the ingredients that go into it. Knowing quality and being an educated, uncompromising shopper not only saves money in the long run but also saves time. Good ingredients actually are easier to prepare. And, of course, the results are that much more satisfying.

Despite the astonishing selection in today's supermarket, reflecting among other things an ever-increasing emphasis on fresh food, astute shoppers must know how to recognize when the zucchini is in good condition, how well the pears will ripen, and whether the melon will be sweet. Often it pays to shop at the farmer's market, the urban greenmarket, or the farm stand up the road; the satisfaction of finding just-picked corn, vine-ripened tomatoes, or apples grown without pesticides more than compensates for the extra trip.

When the great French chef Paul Bocuse talked about *cuisine du marché* (cooking of the market), what he meant was shopping for whatever was of top quality in the market, then planning the menu after selecting the ingredients. It's a discipline worth acquiring. Too many cooks shop the other way around.

These days, if I plan to serve fish, the variety I buy depends entirely on what looks good in the store. That holds true for fruits and vegetables as well. Although this book provides complete menus with recipes, you should feel free to use it as a springboard for developing your own delectable menus, substituting according to what your market offers. Mix and match the dishes from one menu to another, use salmon instead of skate, and don't hesitate to toss some leftover cooked grains into the salad.

Above all, shop in the spirit of Bocuse, with an open mind, ready to vary the shopping list. Be skeptical of the sign that announces the fish is fresh and learn to detect the characteristics of truly fresh fish: the almost translucent sheen and tight musculature, the lack of dryness, sponginess, cracking, or discernible odor. If the recipe calls for monkfish but what the market is selling is not acceptably fresh, you *can* compromise; but do so by selecting another kind of fish or rethinking the menu, *not* by purchasing less than pristine ingredients.

Increasingly, another factor in determining quality is how the food was produced, not just how it might look and taste. Buying organic produce no longer means settling for shriveled carrots, wormy apples, or contorted cucumbers. New, natural methods of controlling pests and fertilizing plants combined with better marketing have shown that farmers do not have to rely on escalating amounts of chemicals to produce sound food.

Whereas fresh mushrooms were once routinely treated with preservatives to keep them white, it has become easy to find untreated ones. Most of the fresh herbs sold in markets today are organically grown. Apples are no longer drugged with the growth regulator, Alar. Frequently today, such foods are also the best tasting and most worth buying and serving. When given the choice, select ingredients that are organically raised—chickens and eggs from a farm, not a factory, meat that has not been treated with hormones or antibiotics, and fish and shellfish from reliable sources.

I'm not a purist when it comes to food and ingredients, but given the choice I will opt for the less processed, less manipulated, more real. I never bother with sugar and fat substitutes, preferring smaller portions of honest food to artificial indulgences. For me, a piece of wonderful cheese on occasion—a nugget of Parmigiano-Reggiano, for example, or some farmhouse cheddar or a properly tangy chèvre—is far superior to a daily dose of some waxlike, relatively tasteless, low-fat, sodium-free pretender.

If the market that is convenient does not carry enough ingredients to satisfy your scrutiny, complain. Talk to the manager, write to the company president. Demand answers and improvements from the businesses and vendors you patronize on a regular basis.

At the same time, you have the responsibility of properly caring for these ingredients in your own kitchen. Knowing how to store them and what the acceptable shelf life may be are just as important as recognizing their quality in the first place. Throughout this book you will find tips about purchasing and storing the ingredients called for in the recipes.

## MENU PLANNING

The meal must strike a balance between flavor and richness. If one dish is made with cream or cheese, others should rely on vegetable mixtures or stock. Hot spices are welcome in one or perhaps two dishes but not in all of them, and nuts should not be included in every course.

The planning must be done with an eye toward providing attractive color and texture contrasts on the plate and from dish to dish. All the menus in this book include some kind of protein, a generous portion of starch or grain, vegetables, and often a salad and fruit.

Convenience and pleasant eating are other considerations. If the main dish has a lovely sauce, be sure to serve some kind of starch or crusty bread to sop it up. Similarly, buffet foods should be manageable, as should cocktail tidbits.

There is no question that dietary considerations affect how we eat these days. The amount of saturated fat on the table has decreased, and the consumption of fresh produce, grains, legumes, and fish continues to rise. Olive oil has replaced butter and shortening in many dishes. Grilling, roasting, and poaching are preferred to frying.

When I plan dinners for the family, more than when I entertain with a dinner for friends, I keep an eye on diet, avoiding large amounts of butter, cream, and eggs. I feel that festive dinner parties are not the time for rigid dieting.

Of course, if certain friends have dietary constraints, I will make every effort to accommodate them in my menu plan. And at the same time I find that lately, my menus for entertaining do involve less butter or cream and fewer eggs, more grains, and more vegetables. I've also found that the use of top-quality nonstick cookware makes it possible to sauté with considerably less fat and occasionally none at all.

Lastly, although I drink regular coffee, I always serve excellent decaffeinated coffee at a dinner party, out of consideration for the many guests who prefer it in the evening. If the decaffeinated coffee is good enough, others will not be disappointed.

In the planning, especially for a more elaborate dinner, bear in mind the scope of your kitchen, the number of burners on your stove, the capacity of your oven, and the timing of dishes that must cook simultaneously. Preparation is easier if it is not necessary to stir-fry two dishes at once. In this book the menus avoid this legerdemain. If two dishes have to bake simultaneously, they do it at the same temperature.

Remember to take the capacity of your serving equipment and tableware into account when planning menus for larger parties.

The more you cook, the more these considerations become second nature. As they do, you will find that preparing dinners at home, whether for family or for friends, becomes easier and more pleasurable than ever.

The exercise of determining the right wine for a particular dish absorbs many connoisseurs. I take a more relaxed approach. As in planning the foods, I strive for balance rather than choosing wine by slavishly following some rule. I usually serve a red wine with poultry, for example, unless the dish is chicken in a cream sauce. Why? Because that's what I like and my family agrees. And I have never had a guest ask for white instead.

The "weight" of the food—that is, how rich or heavily seasoned it is and how elaborate the preparation—affects the choice of wine. A good rule of thumb is the lighter the food, the lighter the wine. Similarly, a casual, inexpensive dinner calls for a relatively informal wine, not a well-aged Bordeaux. When I plan to serve more than one wine, I see to it that the progression of flavors makes sense. The rule is white before red and light before heavy.

The wine suggestions I have made for each menu are just that: suggested guidelines as to category of wine. Within each category there are dozens, if not hundreds, of possible choices, at many prices. Bear in mind that it is never necessary to serve expensive wines. A bottle of wine costing no more than $12 and often less than $10 can be found to complement every menu in this book.

If you serve wine with any frequency, it makes sense to keep several cases on hand. That way you avoid having to make a purchase at the last minute, or possibly running out of wine. It also pays to have a good supply of classic stem glasses.

For a very basic cellar I recommend a case of good-quality sparkling wine (either from California or Spain, or Champagne from France); a case of a light white wine, such as a sauvignon blanc; one of a richer white wine, such as chardonnay; a case of light red wine in the Beaujolais style; and one of a more refined red wine, such as a cabernet sauvignon from California, Australia, Chile, or France, a Rioja from Spain, or a Sangiovese or nebbiolo from Italy.

# HOMESTYLE DINNERS

With the new, relaxed attitude toward entertaining, the distinction between everyday cooking and menus for dinner parties has narrowed. The food that I now serve when friends are coming for dinner——whether at a moment's notice or planned for weeks——bears a striking resemblance to the dishes I serve to my family on a day-to-day basis.

Today, homey cooking is no longer considered inappropriate for a dinner party. Nor is it simply what mother used to make. For me it has gone well beyond the legacy of my own mother, who was a fabulous cook with a great, instinctive sense of flavor. The heritage of family tradition, once the driving force at the kitchen stove, is now but one of many inspirations for the home cook.

Yet in some respects I am no different from good cooks of generations ago. Putting a tureen of wonderful soup on the table, carving a juicy farm-raised chicken burnished to perfection, serving portions of grilled fish fragrant with herbs and olive oil, or cutting into a simple moist cake studded with berries and spooning a dollop of softly whipped cream alongside every serving still makes me glow with pleasure.

Homestyle also suggests a certain pragmatism, always welcome when guests are arriving. Whereas I might devote more time to preparing and cooking for these occasions, I plan well, selecting dishes that can be prepared in advance. I also keep my utensils in mind and plan to use some of the bowls, platters, pitchers, and kitchen oddments I have gathered over years of rummaging in flea markets, antiques shops, and craft bazaars.

There is an infinite range of possibilities with regard to style and menu. But the elements should reflect the personality and taste of the host or hostess. When I feel comfortable, "at home," if you will, with what I serve my guests and how I serve it, I know that will guarantee an evening that is comfortable for them, too. I also choose wines that marry well with the flavors of the food and the style of the dinner.

*Plum and oat-bran Betty,*
*a warm dessert to herald autumn*

# CONTEMPORARY CLASSICS

LENTIL SALAD WITH BEETS
MEDALLIONS OF MONKFISH WITH CAPER BUTTER
QUICK BROCCOLI PUREE
PLUM AND OAT-BRAN BETTY

◆

Lentil salad, fish with caper butter, and brown Betty are simple classics. In this complete and well-balanced menu, they are updated yet still quick to prepare. Lentils, for example, demand a shorter cooking time than other legumes. The broccoli puree calls for just a brief whirl in the food processor, and because the broccoli is cooked until it is soft, the need to time the cooking carefully is eliminated. An unusual one-sided technique gives the fish an invitingly browned coating without overcooking.

The dessert is a homey, crumbly Betty made with the dark purple Italian prune plums of autumn. Apples, pears, even cranberries could be substituted.

Preparation should begin with the lentils and beets for the salad. The dessert can be assembled and baked while the salad ingredients cook. Finishing the salad, preparing the broccoli, and making the fish then follow.

Whether your choice is a sauvignon blanc, a chardonnay, or a pinot blanc, the white wine to accompany this menu should be full-bodied.

## LENTIL SALAD WITH BEETS

*Serves 6*

2 cups lentils, French Le Puy, if available
5 cups water
3 medium beets, about 1 bunch
¼ pound bacon, finely diced
3 tablespoons balsamic vinegar
1 tablespoon Dijon mustard
1 tablespoon extra-virgin olive oil
Salt and freshly ground black pepper

Place the lentils in a large, heavy saucepan, add the water, and bring to a simmer. Cook until the lentils are tender, about 40 minutes. (You may have to skim the surface of the water in the beginning.) Drain the lentils and set aside, covered.

While the lentils are cooking, cut the beet tops down to within an inch of the bulb. Place the beets in a saucepan, cover with water, and simmer until they are tender, about 20 minutes. Drain, peel, and dice the beets, discarding the bit of stem and roots.

Sauté the bacon in a small skillet until it is golden. Remove it from the pan with a slotted spoon. Fold the bacon and diced beets into the lentils.

In a small bowl, beat the vinegar and mustard together, then beat in the oil. Gently mix with the lentils, season to taste with salt and pepper, and serve.

*L*entils come in assorted colors, from green to brown to orange. There are also several varieties, the most select of which are the blackish green ones from France, called Le Puy lentils. These are smaller and not as flat as regular lentils, but they also retain their texture better.

In the markets in France beets are more often sold cooked than raw because they are a common ingredient in French salads, and no one wants to bother with the mess of cooking and peeling. Thus, to substitute canned beets, if convenience demands, would not greatly diminish the quality of the salad.

## MEDALLIONS OF MONKFISH WITH CAPER BUTTER

*M*onkfish, an unattractive bottom-feeder, yields succulent lobsterlike flesh from its tail, the only part that is used. A large monkfish tail can be sliced into boneless "steaks" or thin medallions.

In this recipe they are cooked on one side only, allowing the floured side to brown nicely without overcooking the fish. Flip each slice over onto a warm plate to serve browned side up; the heat of the plate will cook the fish through.

The sauce, a French-bistro classic, can be lightened in terms of saturated fat (but not calories) by using half butter, half olive oil. Do not use all olive oil because the sauce will not brown properly.

### Serves 6

12 monkfish medallions, ½ inch thick (about 2 pounds)
½ cup all-purpose flour
1 teaspoon dry mustard
  Salt and freshly ground pepper
6 tablespoons (¾ stick) unsalted butter, or 3 tablespoons butter and 3 tablespoons extra-virgin olive oil
1 tablespoon finely minced shallots
2 tablespoons drained capers
2 tablespoons extra-virgin olive oil
1 tablespoon lemon juice
1 tablespoon minced fresh parsley
  Lemon wedges, for garnish

Remove any gray membrane from the fish.

Mix the flour and mustard together, then season to taste with salt and pepper. Dip the medallions in the seasoned flour on one side only and arrange on a plate, floured side up.

Melt the butter, or butter-and-oil combination, in a small skillet. Add the shallots and cook over medium heat until both the butter and shallots have browned; do not allow them to blacken. Stir in the capers. Season to taste with salt and pepper, and set aside in the pan.

Heat the olive oil in a large skillet. When very hot, add the fish medallions, floured side down, and sauté until they turn golden, about 30 seconds. Place 2 medallions, uncooked side down, on each of 6 warmed dinner plates.

Briefly reheat the butter sauce, add the lemon juice and parsley, and spoon a little of the sauce over each medallion. Garnish with lemon and serve at once.

## QUICK BROCCOLI PUREE

### Serves 6

**1 bunch broccoli**
**¼ cup plain yogurt**
**Salt and freshly ground black pepper**

Trim the bottom of the broccoli stems. Cut the broccoli into 1-inch pieces and steam or boil them until they are very tender, about 15 minutes. Puree the broccoli in a food processor. Add the yogurt, and season to taste with salt and pepper. Reheat the puree before serving, if necessary.

*B*roccoli, one of those staple year-round vegetables, should have a tightly packed crown of deep gray-green flowerets. Avoid broccoli with signs of yellowing.

Yogurt adds a touch of tartness to the puree without masking the fresh broccoli flavor.

## PLUM AND OAT-BRAN BETTY

### Serves 6

**2 tablespoons unsalted butter, melted**
**2½ pounds Italian prune plums, pitted and halved**
**¾ cup oat bran**
**1 cup dark brown sugar, packed**
**1 teaspoon ground cinnamon**
**4 tablespoons (½ stick) unsalted butter, softened**
**Whipped cream, heavy cream, or ice cream (optional)**

Preheat the oven to 350°F. Grease a 5- or 6-cup baking dish with some of the melted butter.

Toss the plums in a bowl with the remaining melted butter, ¼ cup of the oat bran, ½ cup of the brown sugar, and ½ teaspoon cinnamon. Spread in the baking pan.

Using a fork, pastry blender, or food processor, combine the remaining oat bran, sugar, and cinnamon with the soft butter until crumbly. Spread over the plums in the baking pan.

Bake for about 40 minutes, or until the top has browned, the filling is bubbling, and the aroma is irresistible. Allow to cool until just warm, then serve with whipped cream, heavy cream, or ice cream, if desired.

*D*espite the oat bran in the topping, this dessert is not for dieters, nor will it help lower cholesterol, since it also contains plenty of butter. Still, it is delicious and provides a reason to keep oat bran on hand. When Italian prune plums are out of season, the Betty can be made with tart apples, or even pears, that have been peeled, cored, and sliced in thick chunks, or with a combination of apples and cranberries. You will need six to seven apples or pears; two cups of cranberries will take the place of half the apples.

# BRIGHT SUMMER SALADS FOR SIX

CAESARED GREEN BEAN SALAD
STEAKHOUSE FISH SALAD
ROASTED POTATO SALAD
CORN ON THE COB WITH CURRY BUTTER
CORNMEAL STRAWBERRY SHORTCAKES

◆

This menu is a delight for a summer dinner party, with a number of lusty crowd-pleasing flavors and dishes that take advantage of the seasonal bounty. Since everything but the corn is served at room temperature, the food can be prepared several hours in advance and the cook is spared last-minute stove duty.

The corn on the cob, offered as a separate course, has a slight adornment in its curry butter. I call the main course a steakhouse salad because it combines a meaty fish with onions, tomatoes, and Worcestershire sauce in a typical steakhouse preparation. A Caesar dressing flavors the green beans, herb-roasted potatoes make a slightly unconventional potato salad, and the classic strawberry shortcake is given a novel turn with the addition of cornmeal to the biscuits.

Swordfish and tuna are so substantial they need a red wine. A straightforward California cabernet sauvignon, merlot, or blend would be the wine to accompany this menu.

## CAESARED GREEN BEAN SALAD

*Serves 6*

1 cup diced Italian or French bread
1 pound fresh green beans, trimmed
2 tablespoons sherry vinegar
2 teaspoons Worcestershire sauce
1 large egg yolk or 1 tablespoon mayonnaise
⅓ cup extra-virgin olive oil
　Salt and freshly ground black pepper
2 tablespoons freshly grated Parmesan cheese

Spread the bread on a foil-lined broiling pan and toast under the broiler a minute or so until it is lightly browned. Set aside.

Steam the green beans for 3 to 4 minutes, until crisp-tender but still bright. Rinse under cold water and dry on paper towels. Arrange in a serving dish.

Beat the vinegar, Worcestershire sauce, and egg yolk or mayonnaise together in a small bowl. Beat in the olive oil until the mixture has thickened and is creamy. Season with salt and pepper.

Scatter the toast cubes over the beans, then pour the dressing evenly over both. Sprinkle with cheese. Serve at room temperature.

*The Caesar salad, invented by Caesar Cardini, a restaurateur in Tijuana, Mexico, in 1924, is back in style. The original recipe calls for raw or coddled egg yolk, but the risk of salmonella from consuming uncooked or undercooked eggs has made many people fearful of preparing it the classic way. If you are uneasy about using the raw egg, substitute a tablespoon of commercial mayonnaise. This recipe does not call for anchovies because their characteristic flavor in the original came from the Worcestershire sauce.*

## STEAKHOUSE FISH SALAD

*Serves 6*

2 pounds fresh swordfish steaks, 1 inch thick
6 tablespoons extra-virgin olive oil
36 cherry tomatoes, halved
1 red onion, thinly sliced and separated into rings
3 tablespoons finely chopped pitted Niçoise-style black olives
2 tablespoons Worcestershire sauce
1½ tablespoons Dijon mustard
1½ tablespoons red wine vinegar
Salt
Coarsely ground black pepper

Trim any skin and dark flesh from the fish. Brush fish with 1 tablespoon of the olive oil. Heat a heavy cast-iron skillet and sear the fish on each side so it browns on the outside but remains quite rare in the middle. This should take about 5 minutes. Alternatively, the fish can be grilled or broiled, but do not overcook. Allow the fish to cool, then slice it across the grain about ½ inch thick. Cut the slices into inch-long pieces. Place in a salad bowl or on a platter with the tomatoes, onion, and olives.

Mix the Worcestershire sauce, mustard, and vinegar in a bowl. Beat in the remaining oil. Season with salt and a generous amount of pepper. Pour the dressing over the fish and vegetables, and toss lightly. Allow to marinate 45 minutes to 1 hour before serving.

*The meatiness of swordfish suggests using it in a lusty salad fortified with the strong flavors of black olives, onion, Worcestershire, and mustard. The ingredients can be prepared in advance but should not be combined more than one hour before serving or the fresh flavor will fade. Salmon or tuna steak can be substituted for the swordfish.*

*Steakhouse fish salad with onions and tomatoes anchors a summer dinner.*

*T*here must be hundreds of ways to make potato salad. On fashionable tables the traditional creamy style long ago yielded to one dressed with a vinaigrette, and plain peeled and sliced potatoes were abandoned in favor of unpeeled red-skinned new potatoes. Recently salads made with herb-flecked roasted potatoes have claimed the spotlight.

## ROASTED POTATO SALAD

### Serves 6

2½ **pounds new potatoes, scrubbed**
1 **garlic clove, minced**
6 **tablespoons extra-virgin olive oil**
**Salt and freshly ground black pepper**
1½ **tablespoons red wine vinegar**
1 **tablespoon Dijon mustard**
2 **teaspoons chopped chives**

Preheat the oven to 425°F.

Cut the potatoes in 1½-inch chunks. Place them in a baking dish that will hold them in a single layer. Toss them with garlic and 3 tablespoons of the oil. Season with salt and a generous amount of pepper.

Roast for about 30 minutes, moving them around in the pan once or twice during baking to brown all sides.

Beat the vinegar and mustard together and beat in the remaining oil. Transfer the potatoes to a bowl and toss with the dressing. Sprinkle with chives; serve warm.

## CORN ON THE COB WITH CURRY BUTTER

### Serves 6

6 **tablespoons (¾ stick) unsalted butter**
1½ **teaspoons curry powder**
12 **ears fresh corn**
**Salt and freshly ground black pepper**

*I*n our house there is very little fooling around when it comes to summer corn on the cob, fresh from a farm. We serve it in abundant quantities, and often as a separate first course, even at dinner parties. Seasoning the butter with curry is a nod to invention.

Using a fork or a food processor, cream the butter and curry powder together. Reshape into a log and wrap tightly in plastic wrap. Refrigerate until firm.

Shuck the corn. Bring a large pot of water to a boil, add the corn, and cover. When the water returns to a boil remove the pot from the heat. Serve the corn within 20 minutes with the curry butter, salt, and pepper.

## CORNMEAL STRAWBERRY SHORTCAKES

*Serves 6*

1⅓ cups all-purpose flour
½ cup yellow cornmeal
4 teaspoons baking powder
Pinch of salt
3 tablespoons granulated sugar
½ cup (1 stick) cold unsalted butter, in pieces
1 large egg, lightly beaten
½ cup buttermilk
1 quart strawberries, hulled and halved
Superfine sugar
1 tablespoon kirsch
1½ cups heavy cream
2 tablespoons confectioners' sugar

*Cornmeal in the dough gives these biscuits a pleasant crunch. Even though the biscuits are fairly thin, they split easily with a sharp knife.*

Preheat the oven to 450°F.

Combine the flour, cornmeal, baking powder, salt, and granulated sugar in a food processor and process to blend. Add the butter and pulse until the mixture is uniformly crumbly. Transfer to a mixing bowl.

Using a fork or your fingertips, lightly stir in the egg and buttermilk, moistening the ingredients enough so they can be gathered together to form a ball of soft dough.

On a lightly floured board pat the dough until it is uniformly ½ inch thick. Cut into six 4-inch rounds. Place the dough rounds on a foil-covered baking sheet and bake until just beginning to brown on top, 14 to 15 minutes. Remove from the oven, and cool on racks.

Place the strawberries in a bowl and sweeten to taste with the superfine sugar. Add the kirsch and macerate for about 1 hour. Whip the cream with 1 tablespoon of the confectioners' sugar.

To serve, split the shortcakes. Spread the bottom halves with some of the whipped cream and top with the strawberries. Spread the undersides of the top halves with the rest of the cream, and place the tops onto the cakes. Dust the tops with sifted confectioners' sugar before serving.

# CURRY, THAI STYLE

JICAMA, CARROT, AND
WATERCRESS SALAD
THAI CHICKEN CURRY
CITRUS TERRINE WITH RUM

◆

Despite the exotic roster of dishes, this menu is quick to prepare. Except for a couple of the ingredients in the chicken curry, it requires only a trip to the supermarket. The dessert calls for advance preparation, but once it has been taken care of, preferably the night before, the menu becomes suitable for a weekday evening after work.

Prepare the first course and the rice. While the rice is cooking, the curry, which takes only about 10 minutes, can be prepared so the two dishes are ready to serve together.

Beer, a fruity white wine such as riesling, or even a rosé or blush wine with a touch of sweetness would best complement this dinner.

*Thai chicken curry, stir-fried and seasoned with ginger,*
*chili, and coconut milk*

## JICAMA, CARROT, AND WATERCRESS SALAD

*Unless your market has small jicama, chances are you will not use an entire one for this recipe. Keep the remainder wrapped in plastic in the refrigerator and use it raw in other salads or slivered in stir-fries.*

*Serves 6*

1 pound jicama, peeled
2 medium carrots, peeled
1 small bunch watercress
   Juice of 2 limes
2 tablespoons rice vinegar
3 tablespoons peanut oil
   Hot red pepper flakes to taste

Cut the jicama into thin slivers and place in a salad bowl. Coarsely grate the carrots and add to the bowl.

Rinse the watercress, remove any large stems, and add the leaves to the bowl.

Combine the remaining ingredients in a small bowl, pour over the salad, and toss.

## THAI CHICKEN CURRY

*This recipe was adapted and simplified from one given to me by Yannick Cam, the owner and chef of Le Pavillon in Washington, D.C. The first time I tried it I was astonished at how quick it was to prepare and how much mouth-filling flavor it provided. Shrimp, fish, or strips of beef can be substituted for the chicken. The recipe can easily be doubled.*

*Serves 6*

2 slices fresh ginger the size of a quarter, peeled
2 tablespoons fresh lemon grass, or ½ tablespoon dried
2 teaspoons hot red pepper flakes
2 teaspoons ground cardamom
2 teaspoons ground coriander
2 teaspoons ground cumin
1 tablespoon Thai shrimp paste or anchovy paste
½ tablespoon black peppercorns
2 tablespoons finely minced shallots
2 tablespoons peanut oil
1½ pounds skinless and boneless chicken breasts, cut in narrow strips
12 ounces canned unsweetened coconut milk
½ teaspoon grated lime rind
2 cups steamed long-grain rice (white or brown)

Place the ginger, lemon grass, red pepper flakes, cardamom, coriander, cumin, shrimp or anchovy paste, peppercorns, and shallots in a blender or a food processor and process to make a paste.

Heat the oil in a large skillet, add the spice paste, sauté a minute or two, then add the chicken and stir-fry until it begins to turn white. Add the coconut milk and lime rind. Bring to a simmer and continue to cook, stirring, until the chicken is cooked through, about 8 minutes more. Serve at once with steamed rice.

## CITRUS TERRINE WITH RUM

*Serves 6*

1 **large pink or ruby red grapefruit**
1 **large white grapefruit**
6 **juice oranges**
2 **packages unflavored gelatin**
3 **tablespoons white rum**

Peel the grapefruit and oranges, removing all traces of white pith. Remove the segments from the membranes that enclose them with a sharp paring knife. Hold the fruit over a bowl as you do this to catch the juices, and squeeze any juice out of the membrane over the fruit. Remove any seeds. You should have 2 cups of fruit segments.

Arrange the segments in a 3-cup glass, ceramic, or stainless-steel terrine.

Combine the juices in a saucepan. Stir in the gelatin. Heat, stirring, just until the gelatin has dissolved; the juice should not come to a simmer. Add the rum. Pour the juice over the fruit in the terrine, cover, and refrigerate until set, at least 8 hours or overnight.

To serve, run a knife along the sides of the terrine, then unmold it onto a platter. It should come out of the mold easily; if not, briefly hold a towel wrung out in hot water on the bottom of the terrine.

*Can any book that deals with American home cooking ignore the Jell-O mold? Today even this cliché, the very opposite of what serious cooks stand for, has been dusted off, spruced up, and recast in stylish terms. More than one pastry chef in a top restaurant has devised a "citrus terrine," simply a gelatin and fruit mold with relatively little gelatin in proportion to fruit, that substitutes fresh orange and grapefruit segments for the traditional canned fruit cocktail. This recipe is adapted from one that was created by Paula Smith at Alison's on Dominick Street in New York.*

# AN ELEGANT DINNER FOR FOUR

RED PEPPER GAZPACHO
BROILED LOBSTERS WITH BRANDY AND BUTTER
SALAD OF PEAS, FLAGEOLETS, AND LETTUCE
LEMON-BLUEBERRY CUSTARD SOUFFLÉ

◆

I t's time to splurge. This dinner for four calls for good-size lobsters, an indulgence requiring liberal budgetary guidelines. The preparation also involves an expenditure of time for the careful peeling of the peppers. The end result is bright and balanced, at once rich and refreshing.

The salad requires advance preparation, as does the gazpacho, which needs chilling. The broiling of the lobsters, however, should be done in an interlude between the first and main courses.

Dessert is deliberately light, a simple refreshment after a rich and filling warm-weather dinner.

A full-bodied vintage Champagne would not be out of place with this dinner, nor would a fine California chardonnay from Sonoma County. Serve a luxurious white Burgundy such as Meursault if the budget allows, a St. Aubin or Pernand-Vergelesses if it does not.

*The dazzling vermillion of the red pepper gazpacho is set against
stark black and white for a stunning color contrast.*

## RED PEPPER GAZPACHO

*Serves 4*

2 pounds red bell peppers
1 small green bell pepper
1 small onion, chopped
2 garlic cloves
2 medium cucumbers, peeled, seeded, and
    chopped
¼ cup red wine vinegar
3 tablespoons extra-virgin olive oil
1 cup ice water
    Salt and freshly ground black pepper
1 tablespoon minced fresh basil

*To avoid unpleasant bits of skin when peppers are pu-reed, as in this cold soup, the peppers must either be peeled or the mixture sieved. I chose to peel the peppers because charring the skin to make it flake off adds a hint of smokey flavor. To avoid peeling them for this recipe you could steam them until soft, puree them, and sieve the puree before adding the other ingredients.*

Grill the red and green peppers over an open flame or under the broiler until well charred and fairly soft. Place in a plastic bag to steam, then rinse to rub off the skin. Seed and chop the peppers.

In a food processor puree the peppers along with the onion, garlic, and cucumbers. Remove the puree to a bowl. Add the vinegar, olive oil, and ice water. Stir, then season with salt and pepper to taste. Chill.

Served chilled garnished with basil.

## BROILED LOBSTERS WITH BRANDY AND BUTTER

*Serves 4*

4 lobsters, 1½ to 2 pounds each, preferably female
¼ cup brandy or Cognac
4 tablespoons (½ stick) lightly salted butter,
    melted
    Freshly ground white pepper

*I usually prefer to steam lob-sters, but for festive occasions this recipe is a little more special. It is the way Gilbert Le Coze, chef and owner of the famous seafood restaurant Le Bernardin in New York, prepares lobsters.*

Split the lobsters in half lengthwise or have your fish market split them. Do not crack the claws.

Brush the lobster meat with the brandy or Cognac and set aside while the broiler is preheating.

Preheat the broiler. Place the lobsters in a roasting pan and brush with butter. Broil the lobsters about 4 inches from the source of heat for about 15 minutes, or just until the shells turn red, the flesh turns opaque, and any coral and tomally are no longer black in color. Season with pepper and serve.

## SALAD OF PEAS, FLAGEOLETS, AND LETTUCE

### Serves 4

½ cup dried flageolets
1 cup shelled fresh green peas (about 1 pound in the shell)
   Salt and freshly ground black pepper
3 garlic cloves, minced
2 tablespoons fresh rosemary leaves
¼ cup extra-virgin olive oil
½ cup very finely shredded iceberg lettuce

Place the flageolets in a saucepan and cover to a depth of 2 inches with cold water. Soak for at least 4 hours or overnight.

Rinse and drain the beans. Cover again with water to a depth of 2 inches. Bring to a simmer and cook gently for about 45 minutes, or until the beans are tender, adding a little more water if necessary. In the beginning of the cooking you may have to skim some foam from the surface. Drain the cooked flageolets.

While the flageolets are cooking, place the peas in water to cover and cook until they are tender, about 2 minutes. Drain.

Mix the flageolets and peas in a bowl. Season with salt and pepper. Fold in the garlic, rosemary, and olive oil. Fold in the lettuce and serve.

*The subtle shades of green in this recipe provide a beautiful counterpoint to the red and white of the lobsters.*

*Flageolets are perhaps the most delicate of all legumes. They are about half an inch long when dried and pale celadon in color. If fresh peas are not available, just omit them and increase the amount of flageolets to ¾ cup; frozen peas do not make an acceptable substitute. Iceberg lettuce, rather than a softer-leaved variety, stands up best in this salad. Use the green outer leaves.*

## LEMON-BLUEBERRY CUSTARD SOUFFLÉ

*Some homey desserts are so old-fashioned that they have nearly been forgotten. But they are among the easiest and most engaging baked desserts to make, infinitely variable, attractive to serve, and lush to consume. One of these is a custard soufflé that separates as it bakes, so the creamy custard stays on the bottom while an airy, cakey topping forms over it.*

*Lemon is a particularly successful flavor. And in summer, with blueberries added, the color contrast is stunning.*

*Serves 4*

3 tablespoons butter
1 cup blueberries
2 large eggs, separated
⅔ cup sugar
¼ cup lemon juice
1 tablespoon grated lemon rind
2 tablespoons flour
1 cup light cream
Pinch of salt
Confectioners' sugar

Preheat the oven to 350°F. Use 1 tablespoon of the butter to grease an attractive 3½- to 4-cup baking dish about 1½ inches deep (an 8-inch porcelain quiche pan is excellent), or four individual 6-ounce soufflé dishes. Set the prepared baking dish or dishes into a larger pan.

Spread the blueberries in the bottom of the dish or dishes.

Beat the egg yolks until light. Beat in the sugar and remaining butter until the mixture is creamy. Beat in the lemon juice, rind, and flour, then whisk in the cream. Beat the egg whites with the salt until they are stiff but not dry. Fold the beaten egg whites into the egg yolk mixture and pour the batter over the blueberries in the baking dish or dishes.

Pour boiling water into the pan holding the baking dish or dishes so the water comes halfway up the side of the dish or dishes. Place in the oven and bake about 40 minutes, until the top is puffed and golden brown. Remove from the oven and allow to cool to room temperature before serving. Dust with sifted confectioners' sugar.

# HOMEY FAVORITES FOR FALL

WARM BISTRO SALAD
HERB-ROASTED CHICKEN
HONEST MASHED POTATOES
CHUNKY CARROTS
PRUNE AND APPLE BATTER CAKE

◆

Chicken, especially a well-burnished, juicy roast chicken with crackling skin, provides a familiar anchor for an old-fashioned American dinner. Mashed potatoes enhance this sense of hominess as do chunks of carrots, cooked so their natural sweetness creates a light glaze.

The first course, a salad of wilted greens with a warm bacon dressing, and the dessert, a quick, flanlike cake of prunes and apples, are inspired by French bourgeois cooking. Like the herb seasoning tucked under the skin of the chicken, they give this menu the touch of sophistication that we have come to expect today.

To prepare this menu it is best to begin with the fruit for the dessert. After that, timing the menu depends on the chicken; once it is in the oven the rest of the dinner can be assembled. The chicken should have finished roasting and the dessert placed in the oven (with the temperature increased slightly) as soon as the salad is ready to go on the table.

With chicken roasted in this fashion my preference is for a light red wine such as Beaujolais, instead of white wine.

## WARM BISTRO SALAD

*Serves 6*

3 tablespoons extra-virgin olive oil
6 ounces country-style slab bacon, cut in small chunks
4½ tablespoons sherry vinegar
2 tablespoons grainy mustard
2 Belgian endive, sliced
1 bunch watercress, rinsed, dried, large stems removed
2 bunches arugula, rinsed, dried, large stems removed
1 small head frisée lettuce, or the light center leaves of 1 head chicory (curly endive), rinsed and dried
Freshly ground black pepper

*Selecting salad greens is a matter not only of what is presentable in the market but how well the leaves complement the dressing. This salad, with its warm and lusty dressing, calls for sturdy greens that will not wilt. Frisée or chicory are the best choice, and escarole or romaine are better than delicate leaf lettuces. If you use chicory, remember that the lighter inner leaves are the least bitter.*

*To omit the bacon, start with three tablespoons olive oil in the pan, then add another five tablespoons after the vinegar and mustard are stirred in.*

Heat 1 tablespoon of the olive oil in a heavy skillet. (Do not use an aluminum or iron skillet.) Sauté the bacon until golden (approximately 5 minutes), and then transfer to absorbent paper. Pour the fat from the skillet into a small heatproof container and reserve.

Add the vinegar to the skillet and heat briefly, scraping the pan. Remove from the heat and stir in the mustard, then return the reserved bacon and fat to the pan. Add the remaining olive oil.

Tear all the greens into bite-size pieces and place in a glass or ceramic salad bowl. Just before serving reheat the dressing, pour over the salad, and toss. Season to taste with pepper and serve.

## HERB-ROASTED CHICKEN

*Serves 6*

2 tablespoons chopped fresh parsley
1 tablespoon fresh thyme leaves
½ tablespoon fresh tarragon leaves
1 garlic clove
2 tablespoons extra-virgin olive oil
    Salt and freshly ground black pepper
1 roasting chicken, about 4½ to 5 pounds
    Several sprigs fresh parsley
2 medium onions
½ cup dry white wine, chicken stock, or water

Using a knife or food processor, mince the parsley, thyme, tarragon, and garlic together. Mix with 1½ tablespoons of the olive oil. Season to taste with salt and pepper.

Rinse and dry the chicken. Carefully work your fingertips under the skin and spread most of the herb mixture evenly over the flesh. Rub the remaining herb mixture into the cavity of the chicken and rub the remaining olive oil over the outside of the chicken.

Place the sprigs of parsley and one of the onions, quartered, inside the chicken. Tie the legs together with butcher's cord or a strip of cheesecloth, and tuck the wingtips under the back. Preheat the oven to 400°F.

Place the chicken on a rack in a roasting pan. Slice the remaining onion and scatter the slices in the pan. Roast the chicken for 1 hour and 20 minutes, or until the juices run clear when the thigh is pricked with a fork. Transfer the chicken to a carving board.

Heat the wine, stock, or water in a small saucepan and pour it into the roasting pan, stirring and scraping the pan. Strain the contents of the roasting pan into the saucepan and heat. Skim the fat if desired.

Carve the chicken and arrange it on a warm serving platter. Serve the chicken moistened with a little of the sauce, with the rest of the sauce passed alongside.

*In this recipe extra flavor comes from roasting the chicken with a paste of fresh herbs and garlic spread under the skin. I prefer to use the naturally tasty free-range, farm, and kosher chickens that many butchers carry. I feel they are worth the premium prices they fetch, not only for the quality they provide but also because of their reliability; chickens that are not industrially processed are less likely to carry diseases. Be sure to cook any chicken properly, to a temperature of 160°F. (If your chicken has a pop-up timer, it will not have registered because the timers generally are calibrated to 180°F.) When the thigh is pricked, the juices will run clear.*

*Herb-roasted chicken, honest mashed potatoes, and chunky carrots—all fall favorites*

## HONEST MASHED POTATOES

*Of all the homestyle foods, mashed potatoes make me hungriest. For the best results, use plain boiling potatoes and add hot milk to keep the texture light. Then add butter until you think you'll feel guilty. Alternatively, you could use some of the new, golden, naturally buttery-tasting potatoes, such as Yukon Golds or Finnish.*

*Serves 6*

3 pounds boiling potatoes, peeled
Salt
¾ cup hot milk
1 to 4 tablespoons unsalted butter, softened
Freshly ground black pepper

Cut the potatoes into uniform 2-inch chunks. Place in a saucepan, cover with salted water, and bring to a boil. Cook until tender, about 20 minutes. Drain.

Mash the potatoes with a ricer or force them through a coarse sieve. Lightly stir in the milk with a fork, then stir in as much butter as conscience will allow; do not overbeat. Season with salt and pepper. Serve at once.

## CHUNKY CARROTS

*When the natural sugar in the carrots begins to caramelize in the pan it brings a deliciously sweet flavor to this dish, balancing the acid of the lemon. And unlike green vegetables, carrots do not discolor when lemon is added.*

*Serves 6*

8 to 10 medium carrots, about 1 pound
1 tablespoon unsalted butter
1 tablespoon fresh lemon juice
¼ cup water
Salt and cayenne pepper to taste

Peel the carrots and slice them at an angle into 1-inch chunks.

Melt the butter in a medium, heavy saucepan. Add the carrots and toss them in the pan over medium-high heat for about 5 minutes, until they begin to sear. Add the lemon juice and water, lower the heat, cover the pan, and cook until the carrots are tender, about 20 minutes.

Toss the carrots again, season to taste with salt and cayenne pepper, and serve.

## PRUNE AND APPLE BATTER CAKE

*Serves 6*

1½ **cups pitted prunes**
⅓ **cup warmed Cognac or Armagnac**
4 **tablespoons (½ stick) unsalted butter**
1½ **cups apples, peeled, cored, and sliced**
¾ **cup sugar**
¼ **teaspoon ground cinnamon**
1 **tablespoon fresh lemon juice**
½ **cup milk**
2 **large eggs**
½ **cup all-purpose flour**
**Whipped cream or vanilla ice cream (optional)**

*T*his flanlike dessert, a mellow combination of fruit in a custardy batter, is quick to assemble and bake. It's a variation on a provincial French dish called clafoutis, often made with fresh cherries. The French sometimes do not even bother to pit the fruit, but I prefer to take the time to make the dessert easier to eat.

Lately, clafoutis, like mashed potatoes, has appeared on the menus of better restaurants, proving once again the enduring quality of home cooking.

Place the prunes in a bowl, pour the brandy over them, and allow to soak for 20 minutes.

Melt 2 tablespoons of the butter in a heavy skillet, add the apples, and sauté over high heat until the apples are well coated with butter. Add 3 tablespoons of the sugar and continue to sauté until the sugar begins to caramelize in the pan. Add the prunes, Cognac, and cinnamon. Cook, stirring, several minutes longer, until the prunes soften. Stir in the lemon juice and remove from the heat. Set aside.

About 35 minutes before serving time, preheat the oven to 425°F. Place the remaining butter in a 9- or 10-inch round glass or ceramic baking dish. Place the dish in the oven while the oven is preheating to melt the butter.

Place the milk, eggs, flour, and ½ cup sugar in a blender or food processor and process until well mixed.

Make sure the baking dish is well coated with butter. Pour a thin film of the batter in the dish, then spread the prune and apple mixture over the film of batter. Pour the rest of the batter over the fruit. Place the dish in the oven and bake for about 30 minutes, or until the batter is puffed and browned. Sprinkle top with the remaining tablespoon of sugar, and return to the oven for a few minutes, then serve, with whipped cream or ice cream, if desired.

# SUMMERTIME RICHES

SMOKEY RISOTTO

CHERRY TOMATO COMPOTE

FISH FILLETS WITH
GREEN SAUCE

PEACH TATIN CAKE

◆

A fine summertime menu begins with a filling first course, moves on to a lighter, colorful main dish and side dish, and finishes with a sweet fruit dessert. This menu is a perfect example of that philosophy.

The menu also enables the cook to finish all the preparation by the time the dinner is ready to serve, and thus enjoy the meal with the guests. The risotto must be prepared just before serving, but both the fish and the compote are excellent served warm and can be prepared first. The dessert can be baked earlier in the day, but it is best if not refrigerated before serving.

This menu calls for white wine with a balance of acidity and fruit. A Pouilly fumé or a California fumé blanc would complement it beautifully.

*The last-minute addition of smoked mozzarella adds haunting flavor to this classic risotto.*

## SMOKEY RISOTTO

*Serves 6*

5 cups hot, well-seasoned chicken stock
(approximately)
2 tablespoons unsalted butter
1 medium onion, finely chopped
1½ cups Italian Arborio rice
6 ounces smoked mozzarella or smoked scamorza
cheese, finely diced
Freshly ground pepper to taste
Salt (optional)

*A*mericans love the flavor of smoke. Smoked fish, smoked meats, and smoked poultry have become staples of the new American style. This risotto incorporates the hauntingly mellow flavor of smoked mozzarella. It is extremely rich and filling, and it must be served as a separate course not only because of its preparation (it cannot be held warming) but also because of its intensity.

In a heavy medium saucepan, heat the stock to a slow simmer.

Melt the butter in a large, heavy saucepan. Add the onion and cook over medium heat until it is golden, about 6 minutes. Stir in the rice.

Gradually add the stock to the rice, about ½ cup at a time, stirring constantly and adding more stock as each portion is absorbed by the rice. Adjust the heat so the rice and stock cook steadily but gently. After about 20 minutes all the stock should have been added, the rice should be just tender but not soft, and there should be a creamy texture.

Fold in the cheese, remove from the heat, and season with pepper and, if necessary, a pinch or so of salt. Serve at once.

## CHERRY TOMATO COMPOTE

*Serves 6*

2 pints cherry tomatoes, rinsed and halved
2 tablespoons extra-virgin olive oil
2 garlic cloves, minced
1 sun-dried tomato in oil, drained and minced
2 tablespoons balsamic vinegar
3 tablespoons chopped fresh Italian parsley

*W*atch the cherry tomatoes carefully when you prepare this variation on a stir-fry. They are done when they just begin to soften but have not collapsed.

Heat the oil in a heavy skillet. Add the garlic and sauté for a few seconds over medium heat. Stir in the sun-dried tomato and the cherry tomatoes. Toss gently a few minutes. Remove from heat and stir in the vinegar and parsley. Serve warm.

## FISH FILLETS WITH GREEN SAUCE

*Serves 6*

2 tablespoons finely chopped fresh parsley
4 teaspoons capers
2 teaspoons very finely minced onion
1 teaspoon very finely minced garlic
1 tablespoon very finely minced cornichons
⅔ cup extra-virgin olive oil
  Salt
1 medium carrot, peeled
½ stalk celery
1 small onion, cut in half
  Fresh parsley sprigs
3 tablespoons white vinegar
2 pounds blackfish, tilefish, or salmon fillets

Combine the chopped parsley, capers, onion, garlic, and cornichons with 3 tablespoons of the olive oil. Mix well, season to taste with salt, and set aside.

In a saucepan large enough to hold the fish, place the carrot, celery, onion, and a couple of parsley sprigs. Add 3 to 4 cups of water. Season with salt to taste and add the vinegar. Bring to a boil.

Add the fish, and when the water returns to the boil, lower the heat to a simmer and poach the fish gently for 8 to 10 minutes.

Remove from the heat and allow the fish to cool for a few minutes in the poaching liquid, then drain it. Brush the fillets with the remaining olive oil. Stir the green sauce well, then nap the fish with it. Serve at once.

*With the price of popular fish, even cod, escalating to astronomic heights, wise cooks search for new, less-known, and more moderately priced varieties to try. It has been said that blackfish, an Atlantic fish sometimes called tautog or wrasse, may be the monkfish of the 1990s. Its firm texture and mild flavor are indeed similar to tilefish, which can be substituted for it. Salmon fillets are also excellent prepared this way, as are fillets of Pacific rock cod. The green sauce is a wonderful condiment to serve with steamed vegetables, chicken, and boiled beef.*

*T*he tarte des Demoiselles Tatin, an upside-down apple tart that is a specialty of the Loire Valley of France, was made famous by the Tatin sisters, who ran a restaurant in Lamotte-Beuvron. This simplified version substitutes peaches for the apples and replaces the pastry with a thin cake batter, creating a delectably caramelized compromise between an American upside-down cake and the original tarte Tatin.

## PEACH TATIN CAKE

*Serves 6 to 8*

3 large, ripe peaches, pitted, peeled, and sliced ½ inch thick
1¾ cups sugar
⅓ cup water
1 cup all-purpose flour
¾ teaspoon baking powder
¼ teaspoon grated nutmeg
½ cup (1 stick) unsalted butter, softened
3 large eggs
¾ cup crème fraîche

Preheat the oven to 350°F. Butter a 9-inch pie pan. Arrange the peach slices in a pattern in the bottom of the pie pan.

Combine 1 cup of the sugar with the water in a skillet or shallow saucepan. Cook without stirring over medium-high heat until the mixture turns amber. Remove from heat and immediately pour this caramel evenly over the peaches. Set aside.

Sift the flour, baking powder, and nutmeg together and set aside.

Cream the butter with the remaining sugar until fluffy. Beat in the eggs one at a time, then stir in the flour mixture. Spread this batter evenly over the peaches. Bake for 30 minutes or until the cake has nicely browned.

Allow the cake to cool for at least 40 minutes. Run a knife around the sides and invert the cake onto a serving plate set on a cooling rack. If any slices of peach cling to the pan, lift them off gently and replace them on top of the cake. Serve the cake warm or cooled, with crème fraîche on the side.

**Peach Tatin, an upside-down caramel cake**

# A Light Menu for Four

Quick Corn Soup

Stir-Fried Okra

Grilled Mako with
Grilled Tomato and Onion Salsa

Baked Apricots

*Leftover Bonus:* Mako Hash

◆

Corn, okra, fresh apricots, and grilled fish with a tomato salsa put a seasonal summertime spin on this menu. Although canned corn could be substituted for kernels stripped from just-picked cobs, nothing can replace the apricots of June and July.

Because the fish requires a brief sojourn in a marinade, readying this part of the menu should come first on your schedule. Next, put the apricots in to bake, prepare the salsa and the soup, grill the fish, and stir-fry the okra, in that order. The fish is delicious served at room temperature rather than piping hot off the grill, an option that might make assembling the menu more convenient.

My mother used to welcome leftover fish to make into fish cakes. I prefer to turn it into a chunky, peppery hash.

This menu calls for a light red wine—a Dolcetto from Italy or a Beaujolais served slightly chilled.

## QUICK CORN SOUP

*Serves 4*

1 tablespoon unsalted butter
¼ cup finely chopped onion
¼ cup finely chopped green pepper
½ teaspoon ground cumin
½ teaspoon sugar
2 tablespoons fresh bread crumbs
2 cups corn kernels
2 cups milk
Salt and freshly ground black pepper
1 tablespoon minced fresh chives

Melt the butter in a heavy saucepan. Add the onion and green pepper and sauté over medium-low heat until the vegetables are tender, about 8 minutes. Stir in the cumin, sugar, and bread crumbs, and cook for a few minutes longer until all the ingredients are well moistened.

Add the corn and milk. Bring to a simmer and cook for 5 minutes, until the soup thickens slightly. Season with salt and pepper and serve garnished with chives.

*There's no substitute for farm-fresh corn picked that very morning, if you're serving it on the cob. But for cooked dishes either vacuum-packed canned corn or frozen corn kernels are fine. Keep some on hand at all times for soups such as this, or to add to quick breads or muffins, stuffings, or salads. If you have leftover cooked corn on the cob, you can cut the kernels off and freeze them in a plastic container for later use.*

## STIR-FRIED OKRA

*Serves 4*

1 pound fresh okra, the smaller the better
½ tablespoon extra-virgin olive oil
½ teaspoon curry powder
Salt and freshly ground black pepper

Slice the okra about ½ inch thick and discard stem ends.

Heat the oil in a wok or skillet. Add the okra and stir-fry until it is just tender, about 6 minutes. Do not cook it until it is soft.

Add the curry powder and salt and pepper, stir again, and serve.

*Pods of okra contain a gelatinous substance that is released by long cooking, which is why okra is important as a thickener for gumbo. In this recipe the okra is cooked lightly to obtain tenderness without the goo. For people who find cooked okra unpleasant this recipe is a delightful revelation.*

*Grilled mako with grilled salsa, quick corn chowder, and baked apricots on the side*

## GRILLED MAKO WITH GRILLED TOMATO AND ONION SALSA

*Serves 4*

2 pounds mako shark, about 1 inch thick
Juice of 3 limes
½ teaspoon chili powder
⅓ cup extra-virgin olive oil
Salt
Cayenne pepper
2 medium, ripe tomatoes, cut in thick slices
1 large onion, peeled and cut in thick slices
2 tablespoons finely chopped scallion
2 tablespoons minced fresh coriander

*T*hick fish such as this becomes dry if overcooked. One way to test for doneness is to press the fish lightly with your finger; it should yield with a slight resiliency but not feel either mushy, which means it is still too rare, or hard and overcooked. Open the palm of one hand wide and press the ball of flesh at the base of your thumb. That's about how the fish should feel.

Divide the mako into 4 pieces of equal size. Place them in a dish that will hold them in a single layer.

Combine the juice of 2 limes with the chili powder, ¼ cup of the olive oil, and salt and cayenne pepper to taste. Pour over the fish and turn them to coat all sides. Marinate for about 45 minutes.

**40**

Preheat a grill or broiler. Brush the tomato and onion slices with the remaining olive oil and grill or broil them until they just begin to sear. Allow them to cool slightly.

Finely chop the tomato and onion slices and combine with the scallion, coriander, and remaining lime juice in a bowl. Season to taste with salt and cayenne pepper. Set salsa aside.

Grill or broil the fish to the desired degree of doneness, turning once. (It should take about 8 minutes total cooking time for medium.)

Check seasoning of the salsa. Serve the fish topped with the salsa.

## BAKED APRICOTS

*Serves 4*

**8 fresh apricots, the larger the better**
**2 tablespoons unsalted butter**
**2½ tablespoons sugar**
**2 tablespoons brandy**

Preheat the oven to 500°F.

Halve and pit the apricots. Lightly butter a baking dish that will hold the apricot halves in a single layer. Sprinkle the dish with ½ tablespoon of the sugar.

Arrange the apricots, cut side up, in the dish. Sprinkle with remaining sugar, 1 tablespoon of the brandy, and dot with the remaining butter. Place in the oven and bake about 20 minutes, until the apricots begin to brown around the edges.

Remove the apricots from the oven, sprinkle with the remaining brandy, and set aside to cool at least 15 minutes before serving. They can be served warm or at room temperature.

*The season for fresh apricots is limited to about four weeks from mid-June to mid-July. When fresh apricots are in season they are wonderful to use in baking because they are easy to pit, do not require peeling, and do not discolor readily when cut. Look for fruit that has no signs of green, yields slightly to the touch, but has no soft spots. Small apricots may have better flavor and texture than large ones for eating raw, but large ones are best for cooking.*

*Serve any leftover salsa with this hash, which makes an excellent lunch or supper dish with a green salad. This basic hash recipe can also be used with other leftovers—cooked chicken, duck, turkey, beef, lamb, or other kinds of fish. If needed, moisten the hash with some stock or milk.*

## *Leftover Bonus:* MAKO HASH

### *Serves 4*

2 medium to large boiling potatoes, peeled and cut into ½-inch dice

Salt

3 tablespoons vegetable oil or unsalted butter

1 large onion, chopped

1½ cups diced, cooked mako shark or swordfish or other meaty fish

Juice of 1 lemon

Freshly ground black pepper

1 tablespoon minced fresh parsley

1 tablespoon minced scallion

Leftover salsa

Place the potatoes in boiling salted water and cook about 10 minutes, until barely tender. Drain.

Heat the oil in a large, heavy skillet. Add the potatoes and sauté over medium-high heat until they begin to color, about 10 minutes. Add the onion and continue to sauté until the onion and potato are golden, about 5 minutes longer. Fold in the fish and cook for several minutes until heated through. Add the lemon juice and cook a minute or so longer.

Season to taste with salt and pepper, and fold in the parsley and scallion. Serve at once with leftover salsa.

# A Low-Calorie Dinner Party Menu

Hot and Cold Melon
Tabbouleh with Eggplant
Skate with Tomatoes and Olive Oil
Fromage Blanc with Red Fruit Coulis

◆

Except for desserts, I find I'm using less butter and cream in my cooking. I serve more fish, poultry, and lean meats such as game. As a result, I rarely find it necessary to redraft a menu for dieting guests. They can simply refuse the whipped cream on the cake and be virtuous.

But occasionally we entertain friends who are on very serious low-fat regimes. This is a menu for them. From an hors d'oeuvre that must count its calories in the single digits to a main course of fish lightly glossed with fragrant olive oil and ripe tomatoes, served with a vegetable-enriched grain, to a dessert that involves a light, nearly fat-free cheese with lush fresh fruit, this dinner is a dieter's delight.

Although the fish cannot be prepared long in advance, it can wait thirty minutes or so. As with many of my favorite summer menus, nothing must be served piping hot.

In keeping with lowered calories, try a German riesling kabinett with this meal. These wines tend to have only seven or eight percent alcohol (compared with a more typical twelve percent in other white wines). The slight fruitiness of a classic kabinett or even a spätlese complements the flavors in this menu better than the new bone-dry *trocken* wines from Germany, which I think are too austere.

## HOT AND COLD MELON

*Serves 6*

½ **honeydew melon, not too ripe**
**Juice of 1 lime**
1¼ **to 1½ teaspoons pure chili powder**

*On a trip to San Miguel de Allende, my son Robert discovered that melon, cucumbers, and jicama doused with chili powder and lime are sold by street vendors. The honeydew makes an appetite-whetting hors d'oeuvre with calories too few to count.*

Remove the seeds and skin from the melon and cut it into 1-inch chunks. Place in a bowl. Add the lime juice and chili powder; toss to mix. Serve the melon immediately from a bowl with toothpicks on the side, or skewer each piece with a bamboo pick and arrange on a platter.

## TABBOULEH WITH EGGPLANT

*Serves 6*

¾ **to 1 pound eggplant**
1½ **cups boiling water**
1 **cup bulghur wheat**
**Juice of 1½ lemons**
⅓ **cup chopped green bell pepper**
3 **tablespoons minced scallion**
1 **garlic clove, minced**
3 **tablespoons sesame seeds**
3 **tablespoons minced fresh parsley**
2 **tablespoons extra-virgin olive oil**
**Salt and freshly ground black pepper**

*Tabbouleh, the Middle Eastern cracked-wheat salad, is one of those traditional but infinitely variable dishes. In this recipe it is seasoned with chopped eggplant and herbs.*

*The sesame seeds add an extra nutty quality. You can substitute sesame oil for the olive oil if you wish.*

Preheat the oven to 425°F. Place the whole eggplant on a pan or baking sheet and bake until tender, about 45 minutes. When done, set aside to cool.

While the eggplant is baking, pour boiling water over the bulghur and stir in the juice of a lemon. Set aside.

When the eggplant is cool enough to handle, discard the stem and the skin and chop the flesh. Drain the bulghur, pressing out any excess fluid. Combine with the eggplant. Add the remaining ingredients and stir lightly. Season to taste with salt and pepper.

**Hot and cold melon to whet the appetite**

# Skate with Tomatoes and Olive Oil

*Serves 6*

2 pounds boneless skate wings
Juice of 1 lemon
Salt and freshly ground black pepper
5 tablespoons extra-virgin olive oil
2 tablespoons fresh bread crumbs
1 medium onion, chopped
2 garlic cloves, minced
3 ripe, medium tomatoes, chopped
2 tablespoons minced fresh basil

*Skate wings, the triangular appendages of the ray or skate, are another variety of "trash" fish worth investigating. The fish is usually sold as a fillet without its underpinning of cartilage; it has a soft but slightly fibrous texture, a mild flavor, and an attractive, almost ruffled appearance. It cooks very quickly. Leftover skate marinated in a light dressing makes a delicious salad.*

Divide the skate wings into 12 equal portions. Place in a dish, sprinkle with the lemon juice, and season with salt and pepper.

Heat 1 tablespoon of the oil in a heavy skillet, preferably nonstick, add the bread crumbs, and sauté until they are golden. Remove the bread crumbs from the pan, set aside, and wipe the pan.

Heat another tablespoon of the oil in the skillet. Add the onion and sauté over medium heat until it is tender, about 6 minutes. Add the garlic and sauté briefly, then add the tomatoes. Stir the tomatoes into the other ingredients for a minute or two, just enough to warm them without cooking through. Remove the vegetables from the pan.

Add one more tablespoon of oil to the pan and cook the skate over medium heat, about 3 minutes on each side, until just cooked through, the whiter side first. The fish will not take on any color. Arrange the skate on a warm platter or on individual plates.

Return the tomato mixture to the skillet, add the remaining 2 tablespoons of oil, stir, season with salt and pepper, and add the basil. Pour this mixture around the fish. Sprinkle the fish with the bread crumbs and serve.

## FROMAGE BLANC WITH RED FRUIT COULIS

*Serves 6*

1½ quarts buttermilk
2 to 3 tablespoons skim milk (optional)
½ pint fresh raspberries
1 pint fresh strawberries
Sugar

Place the buttermilk in a saucepan and heat gently for about 10 minutes, until a thermometer reads 110° to 115°F. (You can use an instant-read meat thermometer for this.) At this temperature you should see the buttermilk begin to congeal and be surrounded by the whey, a whitish liquid.

Allow the buttermilk to sit undisturbed until it cools. Using a knife, cut down through the curd, making blocks. Line a fine strainer with 2 thicknesses of cheesecloth and place it over a bowl. Using a slotted spoon, ladle the curds out of the saucepan and into the strainer. Allow the cheese to drain for several hours or overnight; the longer it sits the firmer it will be.

When the cheese is the desired consistency, remove it from the strainer and whip it with a fork until smooth. Add a little skim milk to soften the texture, if desired. It should be spreadable, like whipped cream cheese. Refrigerate until ready to serve.

Puree most of the raspberries and strawberries, reserving a few whole berries for garnish. Strain the puree to eliminate the seeds. Sweeten to taste if necessary.

Serve small scoops of the fromage blanc surrounded by some of the fruit coulis and garnish with whole berries.

*Fromage blanc is the French version of cottage cheese. Low in fat like cottage cheese, fromage blanc is very smooth. Cottage cheese pureed in a blender is a viable substitute. Several years ago, when fromage blanc was virtually unavailable here, I began making my own from buttermilk. I passed the technique on to Jacques Torres, the pastry chef at Le Cirque restaurant in New York, and now he makes his own, too.*

*Red fruit, or les fruits rouges in France, is the term for assorted summer berries and cherries. Vary the proportions according to fruit available in the market.*

# A HOMEY CHINESE DINNER

GRILLED MUSHROOMS AND SCALLIONS
WITH SESAME OIL
CHINESE MEATBALLS AND CABBAGE
FIVE-SPICE RICE
PLUMS IN PLUM WINE

◆

Today, the geography of taste has expanded at home as it has in restaurants. Asian touches have become commonplace now that ingredients such as fresh ginger and soy sauce are supermarket staples. The focus of this menu is a hearty casserole of meatballs seasoned with ginger, garlic, and soy sauce, cooked in broth, a good example of Chinese home cooking. It is exotic enough to serve to guests. Although the dish is usually made with pork and served with plain white rice, I have substituted veal for a less heavy taste and added a fragrant anise infusion of five-spice powder to the rice.

The Asian approach carries through the first course, with sesame oil seasoning the grilled vegetables. The plum wine, a Japanese dessert staple, dresses up fresh plums beautifully.

Begin the menu by preparing the casserole. If it is finished before the other courses are ready to go on the table, it can easily be reheated. The dessert should be next on the agenda, followed by the rice and first-course vegetables.

A fruity white wine, such as a dry chenin blanc from California, a Rhine riesling, or an Alsatian gewürztraminer, would be one choice of beverage; beer would be another.

*First-course mushrooms and scallions on the grill*

## GRILLED MUSHROOMS AND SCALLIONS WITH SESAME OIL

*Serves 4 to 6*

**1½ pounds medium to large mushrooms, preferably shiitake**
**1 bunch scallions**
**¼ cup oriental sesame oil**
**Salt and freshly ground black pepper**

Preheat the broiler or grill.

Trim the stems from the mushrooms. Trim the roots from the scallions and peel off their outermost layer. Trim the leaves so the scallions are about 6 inches long.

Brush the mushrooms and scallions with the oil.

Broil or grill the scallions and mushrooms, turning them once, until they are lightly browned, about 5 minutes. Season to taste with salt and pepper and serve.

*Larger, rather than smaller, mushrooms are best for this recipe. Cultivated shiitakes are my first choice, but oyster mushrooms or cultivated white mushrooms can be substituted. Store mushrooms loosely wrapped in paper towels, not plastic, in the refrigerator. Exposure to air may dry them a bit, but they can become limp and rot in plastic.*

## CHINESE MEATBALLS AND CABBAGE

*This recipe is also called Lion's Head because the large meatballs surrounded by frizzles of cabbage resemble a lion with its mane. It is a popular Cantonese dish that is often served for the New Year. The recipe calls for tree ears, a type of fungus that's sold in stores specializing in Asian ingredients and some supermarkets.*

*The finished dish includes enough rich, dark, brothlike sauce to moisten the meatballs, the cabbage, and the rice.*

*Serves 4 to 6*

½ cup dried tree ears (black fungus)
1 cup warm water
2 pounds coarsely ground veal or turkey
1 tablespoon minced scallion
1 tablespoon minced fresh ginger
2 garlic cloves, minced
⅓ cup dark soy sauce
2 tablespoons cornstarch
⅓ cup dry sherry or rice wine
2 tablespoons peanut oil
2½ pounds Chinese cabbage (napa)
1 teaspoon salt
Pinch of sugar

Mix the tree ears and water in a bowl and set aside to soften.

Mix the veal with the scallion, ginger, garlic, and soy sauce. Dissolve the cornstarch in the sherry and mix with the meat. Shape the meat into 8 rounded, loosely packed patties.

Heat the oil in a heavy 3-quart casserole that has a tight-fitting lid, and lightly brown the patties on both sides. Remove them from the casserole.

Slice the cabbage into 1-inch pieces, removing the core. Place it in the casserole. Sprinkle the cabbage with salt and sugar, cover, and cook over low heat for about 15 minutes, until the cabbage begins to wilt. Remove from heat. Drain the tree ears and mix them with the cabbage. Place the meat patties on top of the cabbage.

Cover the casserole and cook over low heat for about 1 hour. Serve the meat, cabbage, and broth in shallow bowls.

## FIVE-SPICE RICE

*Serves 4 to 6*

1 tablespoon vegetable oil or peanut oil
1 teaspoon minced fresh ginger
1 garlic clove, minced
¼ cup finely chopped scallions
2 teaspoons Chinese five-spice powder
1 cup long-grain rice
1⅓ cups chicken stock or water
Salt

Heat the oil in a heavy 2- to 3-quart saucepan. Add the ginger and garlic, and when they begin to sizzle add the scallions. Sauté over medium heat for a few minutes, then stir in the five-spice powder. Stir in the rice, and when the grains are well coated, stir in the stock or water. Bring to a simmer. Add salt to taste if necessary.

Reduce the heat to very low, cover the pan, and cook for 17 minutes, or until all the liquid has been absorbed. Remove the pan from the heat and set aside, covered, for 5 minutes before serving.

*F*ive-spice powder is one of several spice blends used in the cooking of various countries. Like the French quatre épices, Chinese five-spice powder contains black pepper, cinnamon, and cloves. But fennel seeds and star anise give the Chinese blend a decided licorice flavor, whereas the French mix features nutmeg.

With additional chopped scallions and a vinaigrette dressing seasoned with sesame oil, this rice also makes an excellent salad for a summer menu.

## PLUMS IN PLUM WINE

*Serves 6*

2 pounds red and purple plums, ripe but not soft
⅓ cup Chinese plum wine
2 tablespoons very finely minced crystallized
    ginger

If the plums are freestone, you can simply slice each in half and lift out the pit. Otherwise slice each plum not quite in half along both sides of the center pit, releasing the pit.

Cut the pieces of plum into julienne strips. Place in a bowl and toss with the plum wine and the ginger. Serve in goblets.

*D*ousing fruit with a liqueur or wine is an easy means of transforming the simplest dessert into one with considerable style. The garnish, crystallized ginger in this case, helps. Match the fruit and alcohol with care. If you have no plum wine, try just a tablespoon of plum eau-de-vie or Armagnac.

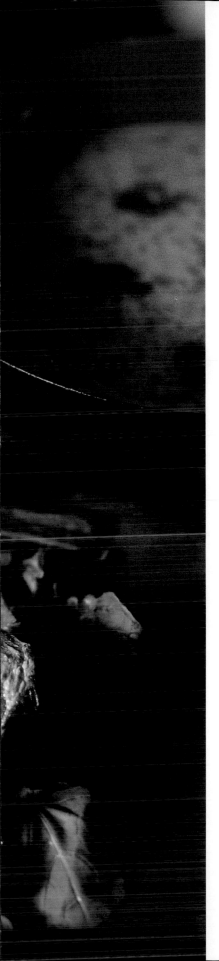

# An Intimate Summer Dinner

CORIANDER SOUP

LAMB CHOP SALAD WITH
BALSAMIC VINEGAR DRESSING

MARINATED MUSHROOM CROSTINI

BELLINI COUPE WITH
SOFT BISCOTTI

◆

I love summer menus that revolve around glorified salads. They are attractive, fresh tasting, and light, and appeal both to me as a cook and to my guests.

The main-course salad and mushroom crostini are virtually finished—the salad greens assembled, the lamb roasted, the mushrooms sautéed, and the bread toasted—before dinner is served. Only slicing the lamb, adding the dressing, and topping the toast with mushrooms remain to be done between courses. Dessert and the chilled soup must be prepared in advance.

The first course calls for a white wine. If you wish to keep it Italian, select an Arneis from the Piedmont or a pinot grigio. Italian red wine such as Barbaresco or a red Bordeaux would best suit the main course.

*Lamb chop salad on a bed of arugula*

## CORIANDER SOUP

*oriander is one of those herbs that has suddenly become fairly widely available. The fresh leaves have a richly pungent aroma and flavor for which there is no substitute. (Ground coriander is made from the seeds and has a different taste entirely.)*

*When using fresh coriander in a recipe such as this it is best to strip the leaves from the stems. If fresh coriander is not available, replace it with fresh watercress. To serve the soup hot use all half-and-half and no yogurt.*

*Serves 4*

1 tablespoon extra-virgin olive oil
½ tablespoon minced fresh ginger
2 garlic cloves, minced
1 teaspoon ground coriander
1½ cups fresh coriander leaves, packed
6 cups chicken stock
1 cup half-and-half and ½ cup plain yogurt
Salt and freshly ground black pepper
Fresh coriander leaves, for garnish

Heat the oil in a large saucepan. Add the ginger and garlic, and sauté until tender but not brown, just a minute or so. Stir in the ground coriander.

Add the coriander leaves and the stock, bring to a simmer, and cook for 10 minutes.

Puree the soup in a food processor or blender. (A blender will produce a finer texture.) You may have to do this in more than one batch.

Chill the puree overnight. Before serving, stir in 1 cup of half-and-half and the yogurt. Season with salt and pepper. Float fresh coriander leaves on each serving.

## LAMB CHOP SALAD WITH BALSAMIC VINEGAR DRESSING

*ack of lamb is an expensive cut, but by making it the centerpiece of a main-course salad, one rack can be stretched to provide four servings. Be sure the rack you buy can be cut into eight ribs.*

*Serves 4*

1 rack of lamb, well trimmed of fat and frenched
½ cup extra-virgin olive oil
2½ tablespoons balsamic vinegar
½ teaspoon Dijon mustard
½ teaspoon minced fresh rosemary
Salt and freshly ground black pepper
¼ pound lamb's lettuce (mâche) or arugula, rinsed and dried

Preheat the oven to 475°F.

Brush the lamb with a little of the olive oil and place in the oven in a shallow baking pan. Roast for 20 minutes (for medium-rare). Remove from the oven.

Heat the vinegar in a small stainless-steel, enamel, or glass saucepan. Remove from the heat, beat in the mustard, then beat in the remaining olive oil. Season with the rosemary, salt, and pepper.

Place the mâche or arugula in a bowl and toss it with all but 2 tablespoons of the dressing. Arrange the greens on a platter or on 4 individual plates.

Slice the lamb into individual chops. Arrange them on the greens and moisten with the remaining dressing.

## MARINATED MUSHROOM CROSTINI

*Serves 4*

1 **large garlic clove, chopped**
5 **tablespoons extra-virgin olive oil**
1 **pound fresh cultivated mushrooms, sliced**
1 **red bell pepper, cored, seeded, and sliced thin**
¼ **cup chopped red onion**
   **Pinch of rosemary, preferably fresh**
2 **tablespoons white wine vinegar**
   **Salt and freshly ground black pepper**
1 **loaf French or Italian bread, sliced thin**
1 **garlic clove, halved**

Lightly sauté the chopped garlic in 4 tablespoons of the olive oil in a large skillet. Add the mushrooms; stir them over medium-high heat until they begin to brown. Add the pepper, onion, and rosemary. Sauté for a minute, then remove from heat and add the vinegar, remaining olive oil, and salt and pepper to taste. Allow the mushrooms to cool. Before serving, lightly toast rounds of bread, rub with the garlic halves, and serve the mushrooms spooned over the bread.

*E*veryday white mushrooms, sautéed and served on rounds of toasted garlic-rubbed bread, are an excellent accompaniment for a salad main course. Although this recipe calls for plain cultivated mushrooms, some other varieties in the market, including oyster mushrooms, shiitakes, portobellos, and chanterelles, could be substituted or used in combination.

## BELLINI COUPE

*Serves 4 to 6*

**4 large peaches, ripe but not soft**
**Juice of 1 lemon**
**Juice of 1 orange**
**3 tablespoons peach-flavored schnapps**
**1 bottle (750 ml) chilled sparkling wine**

*The Bellini is a blend of Champagne and white peach juice, invented by Arrigo Cipriani in his Venetian restaurant, Harry's Bar. This recipe elevates the cocktail to a light but delightfully festive and pretty summer dessert. Marinating the peaches with their pits enhances their flavor.*

Bring a pot of water to a boil and dip in the peaches for 30 seconds to loosen the skins. Rinse the peaches in cold water, then peel them.

Halve the peaches, remove the pits, and place the pits in a bowl. Combine the lemon juice, orange juice, and schnapps, then add to the bowl with the pits. Slice the peaches and add them. Place a sheet of plastic wrap directly onto the surface of the peaches and refrigerate for 2 hours.

To serve, divide the peach slices and the juice among 4 large stemmed goblets (discard the pits). Carefully pour the sparkling wine over the peaches, pouring slowly because the wine will foam up. Serve at once with Soft Biscotti (recipe follows). When the guests have finished eating the peaches, more wine can be added to the goblets for delicious sipping.

## SOFT BISCOTTI

*Makes 24 to 30 cookies*

1¼ cups all-purpose flour
½ cup sugar
  Pinch of salt
¼ teaspoon baking soda
¼ teaspoon baking powder
2 large eggs
1 teaspoon vanilla extract
½ cup unblanched hazelnuts, coarsely chopped

Preheat the oven to 350°F. Cover a baking sheet with parchment paper.

Sift the flour, sugar, salt, baking soda, and baking powder together into a large mixing bowl.

Beat one of the eggs in a small bowl, remove half to another bowl and reserve. Beat the other egg with the half egg in the first bowl, and add the vanilla.

Make a well in the center of the flour mixture, add the egg and vanilla mixture, and using a rubber spatula or your fingers, work the flour into the egg gradually. The mixture will be crumbly at first but will gradually form a soft dough. Allow the dough to rest a few minutes.

Place the dough on a lightly floured surface and flatten it to form a 6-inch square. Scatter the hazelnuts over the dough, then roll the dough up over the nuts. Flatten slightly, then cut in half. With your hands, roll each half into a rope about 9 inches long and 1½ inches in diameter. Place on the baking sheet and brush with the reserved beaten egg.

Bake the rolls 15 to 20 minutes, until lightly golden and firm to the touch. Transfer them to a cutting board and cut on the diagonal into ½-inch-thick slices. Serve while still warm.

*Biscotti are crisp little cookies that are served to dip in sweet dessert wines in Italy. Literally translated, the name biscotti means "cooked twice." The word biscuit also has the same meaning. Traditionally, nut-studded biscotti are returned to the oven for a second baking to crisp them. Unfortunately, some of mine often do not make it that far because we wind up nibbling them while they are still invitingly warm and soft. In fact, the soft biscotti are so appealing I often prepare them that way deliberately. They can bake while the main course is being served, then be sliced and served with the dessert. Any that are uneaten can be put back into the oven for 15 minutes or so, to firm them for longer storage.*

# AN EAST-WEST DINNER FOR SPRING

SCALLION PANCAKES
ASPARAGUS IN GARLIC SAUCE
THREE-GLASS RABBIT
CHILI-SPICED POTATOES
PINEAPPLE-NUT GALETTE

◆

East-West cooking, which combines Asian and American or European techniques, seasonings, and dishes, continues to make news. It may be the way the melting pot has evolved. It exemplifies the fact that fresh ginger, fresh coriander, oriental sesame oil, and various soy sauces have become commonplace enough to encourage cooks to use them in non-Asian fashion. This springtime menu reflects this style.

The scallion pancakes are a relatively straightforward version of the northern Chinese favorite. The three-glass rabbit, based on a Cantonese chicken dish, is strictly homestyle. In place of rice or noodles, potatoes zapped with hot chili are served along with fresh asparagus in a Chinese garlic sauce. And while pineapple is frequently served as dessert with Chinese food, for this menu it has been showered with nuts and baked as a galette on a simple pastry crust.

The asparagus are best if stir-fried at the last minute, but the rest of the menu takes to advance preparation.

A red wine with enough body to stand up to the spice in the menu is best. A French country wine such as Cahors or a California zinfandel are two examples, although a good amber beer makes a suitable alternative.

## SCALLION PANCAKES

*Serves 6*

2¼ cups all-purpose flour
¾ cup hot water
3 tablespoons oriental sesame oil
  Salt
1 cup chopped scallions
2 tablespoons peanut oil

Serve wedges of these scallion pancakes as an hors d'oeuvre, a plated first course, or even as a side dish with a soup and salad supper. Like all pancakes, they are best eaten when freshly made, but they can be kept warm in an oven for about 30 minutes, if necessary.

Place the flour in the work bowl of a food processor and, with the machine running, add the water through the feed tube and process until a ball of dough forms. (The dough can also be mixed by hand.)

Briefly knead the dough, then allow it to rest for 10 minutes. Roll it out about ¼ inch thick, forming a rectangle. Brush the dough with the sesame oil, sprinkle with salt, and scatter the scallions evenly over it.

Roll the dough tightly into a sausage shape, then cut the roll into 6 equal pieces. Pinch the cut sides of each piece closed to form a ball and then flatten each ball by pressing it lightly with a rolling pin, making circles about 6 inches in diameter.

Heat the peanut oil in a heavy 8-inch skillet over medium-high heat. Fry each pancake, turning once to brown both sides lightly. Drain briefly on absorbent paper, then cut each into 6 wedges and serve.

*Three-glass rabbit richly
braised in a clay pot*

## ASPARAGUS IN GARLIC SAUCE

### Serves 6

1½ pounds medium asparagus
1 tablespoon dark soy sauce
3½ tablespoons Chinese oyster sauce
   Pinch of sugar
2 tablespoons rice vinegar
1 tablespoon oriental sesame oil
1 tablespoon vegetable or peanut oil
1 tablespoon finely minced garlic

*Always purchase asparagus spears of equal thickness so they will cook uniformly. Medium to thick asparagus served whole should be peeled, but when the asparagus is sliced, as in this recipe, peeling is not necessary.*

*Dark soy sauce is thicker and not as salty as light, and is used mostly for cooking, not as a table seasoning.*

Snap the ends off the asparagus and slant-cut them into 1-inch lengths. Combine the soy sauce, oyster sauce, sugar, vinegar, and sesame oil in a small bowl.

Heat the oil in a wok or skillet. Add the garlic, then the asparagus, and stir-fry until crisp-tender, 3 to 5 minutes. Pour in the sauce, stir briefly, and serve.

## THREE-GLASS RABBIT

### Serves 6

2 rabbits, about 3 pounds each, preferably fresh, cut into serving pieces
2 tablespoons vegetable or peanut oil
   One 1-inch piece of fresh ginger, peeled and sliced thin
6 garlic cloves, split
2 tablespoons dry sherry
2 tablespoons dark soy sauce
1 teaspoon sugar
1 tablespoon oriental sesame oil
1 tablespoon chopped fresh coriander

*This is an adaptation of a homey Chinese recipe I first sampled in David Keh's restaurant, Pig Heaven. He called it "three glass" because originally it called for a glass of soy sauce, a glass of wine, and a glass of water. For this rabbit dish I have eliminated the water and altered the proportions somewhat, but the spirit is the same.*

*Prepare this dish in a clay casserole if you have one. If not, sub-*

Presoak a clay pot for 30 minutes in cold water. While it is soaking, rinse and dry the rabbit pieces.

Heat the oil in a large, heavy skillet, add the rabbit, and brown pieces lightly on all sides over medium-high heat, for about 10 minutes. Remove the rabbit and stir in the ginger and garlic. Sauté for about 30 seconds.

Dry the clay pot, then transfer the contents of the pan to the pot. Add the rabbit and the remaining ingredients except the coriander.

Cover the pot and place in the oven. Turn the oven to 400°F. and bake for 45 minutes. Check once during baking to make sure there is still some liquid in the pot. Add a little water if necessary. Garnish with coriander and serve directly from the pot.

*stitute an ovenproof casserole, browning the rabbit and sautéing the other ingredients directly in the casserole. Reduce the baking time to 35 minutes.*

## CHILI-SPICED POTATOES

*Serves 6*

3 pounds boiling potatoes, peeled
Salt to taste
¼ cup vegetable or peanut oil
1 medium red onion, chopped
2 fresh jalapeño peppers, seeded and minced
Freshly ground black pepper
3 tablespoons chopped fresh coriander

Cut the potatoes into pieces about 1 inch × ½ inch × ½ inch. Place in a pot of salted water and parboil until almost tender, about 10 minutes. Drain thoroughly.

Heat the oil in a heavy skillet, preferably nonstick. Add the potatoes and sauté about 10 minutes, or until they are barely beginning to take on color. Stir in the onion and jalapeño pepper and continue to sauté another 10 to 15 minutes, stirring occasionally, until the onion is tender and the potatoes are lightly browned. Season to taste with salt and pepper, fold in the coriander, and serve.

*Parboiling the potatoes makes it possible to sauté them quickly and without their sticking together. The nonstick pan does the rest.*

*When nonstick pans first came on the market in the 1960s, they were meant to be used without butter, oil, or shortening. But they also make sauté jobs easier when oil is used. A nonstick pan is especially useful when sautéing potatoes so you can move them around without causing them to break.*

## PINEAPPLE-NUT GALETTE

*Serves 4 to 6*

2 **cups shelled walnuts or pecans**
¾ **cup all-purpose flour**
  **Pinch of salt**
6 **tablespoons (¾ stick) cold unsalted butter**
3 **tablespoons ice water (approximately)**
¾ **cup light brown sugar, packed**
½ **fresh pineapple, peeled and cored**
2 **tablespoons unsalted butter, melted**

Preheat the oven to 425°F.

Chop the nuts fairly fine in a food processor. Remove 1 cup and reserve. To the remaining nuts, add the flour and salt, and process until the nuts are finely ground. Dice the cold butter and add it to the food processor. Pulse until the butter is about the size of lentils. With the machine running, add enough of the ice water for the mixture to begin to come together and form a ball. The dough should be soft but not sticky. Transfer the dough from the food processor to a floured work surface.

Pat the dough into a circle about ½ inch thick. Place it in an 8- or a 9-inch pan with a removable bottom, and press it evenly into the pan. Mix the reserved nuts with the brown sugar and sprinkle half this mixture over the dough. Slice the pineapple thin and arrange the slices over the nut mixture. Sprinkle the remaining nut mixture over the pineapple and drizzle with the melted butter.

Bake for about 40 minutes, or until the pastry and topping have browned. Allow to cool at least 30 minutes before serving, but do not refrigerate before serving.

*F*ew people realize that a pineapple stops ripening the moment it's picked; don't expect a pineapple to ripen at home. The ease with which the leaves can be pulled out is not a good indication of ripeness. When you select a pineapple look for one that has a pineappley fragrance at the base, with no obvious bruises and skin more yellow than green. Hawaiian pineapples, which are tall and oval, are usually of better quality than the smaller, more rounded Caribbean variety.

# A BASQUE FISH DINNER

HERBED MUSSELS
WARM ZUCCHINI SALAD
STEAMED NEW POTATOES WITH BACON
BASQUE-STYLE FISH
BITTER CHOCOLATE CREAM WITH RASPBERRIES

◆

With its earthy blend of flavors and seasonings, plus the special treat of a sophisticated dessert, this menu represents home cooking with flair and surprise. The mussels are delicious morsels that are excellent to pass with an apéritif or serve at the table. (Careful planning results in a bonus meal of steamed mussels the day before.)

The main dish is unusual—so much so that I could not wait to try it when I happened on the recipe. It is excellent for entertaining because the fish can be seared more lightly than the recipe specifies and kept covered in a barely warm oven until the broth is poured over it just before serving. The bacon-flavored potatoes should be passed alongside but are meant to be placed on the same plate. A zucchini salad, no more than a quick stir-fry served warm, should be served alongside. It can be prepared before the fish and kept loosely covered.

The dessert and the mussels are the only parts of this meal that call for advance preparation; the rest can be pulled together in forty-five minutes or so.

I like a clean-tasting sauvignon blanc with this menu. A light chardonnay such as a Chablis would also be delicious.

## HERBED MUSSELS

*I* prefer medium-size mussels to very large ones because they usually have better flavor. Because the mussels must cool completely after steaming, I often find it more convenient to prepare them the night before. I like to double the amount of mussels and make a quick supper of the steamed mussels one evening, leaving the leftovers for the first course of this menu.

*Serves 4*

1 tablespoon finely minced shallots
1 tablespoon unsalted butter
1 cup fruity white wine, such as a dry Riesling
1 pound medium mussels, scrubbed and debearded
⅓ cup mayonnaise
1 teaspoon grated lemon rind
1 tablespoon mixed finely minced fresh herbs, such as chervil, tarragon, parsley, basil, dill

In a pot of at least 3-quart capacity sauté the shallots in the butter until they are soft but not brown. Add the wine, bring to a boil, then add the mussels and cook until they have opened, about 10 minutes. Remove the mussels from the pot with a slotted spoon, draining them well, and transfer to a bowl. Cover the mussels tightly and allow to cool to room temperature. Reserve the broth to use in fish stock or soups; it can be frozen.

Shuck the mussels, discarding any that have not opened and reserving a single shell for each one. Refrigerate the mussels and the reserved shells separately.

Just before serving, mix the mayonnaise with the lemon rind and herbs. Fold the mixture into the mussels, coating them well. Place a mussel on each shell half, then arrange them on a serving platter or on individual plates and serve.

## WARM ZUCCHINI SALAD

*Z* ucchini, quickly stir-fried until barely wilted, then splashed with a bit of tangy dressing and showered with scallions, is excellent served warm as a salad.

*Serves 4*

3 tablespoons extra-virgin olive oil
1 pound small zucchini (5 to 6 inches long), sliced thin
½ teaspoon coarse salt
Juice of ½ lemon
2 tablespoons chopped scallions

Heat the oil in a wok or skillet. Add the zucchini and stir-fry for about 1 minute, just until the zucchini begins to look moist and lose its rawness. It should still be crisp. Add the salt and the lemon juice and remove from the heat. Toss with the scallions and transfer to a serving dish. Serve while still warm.

## STEAMED NEW POTATOES WITH BACON

*Serves 4 to 6*

2 pounds small new potatoes, peeled
¼ pound thick-sliced bacon
2 tablespoons minced shallots
2 tablespoons white wine vinegar
Salt and freshly ground black pepper
1 tablespoon minced fresh parsley

Steam the potatoes until tender, about 20 minutes. While the potatoes are steaming, fry the bacon in a skillet over medium heat, until it is golden. With a slotted spoon, remove the bacon from the pan, reserving the bacon fat, and drain it on absorbent paper. When cool, chop the bacon and set aside.

Add the shallots to the bacon fat in the skillet and sauté until they just begin to brown, about 2 minutes. Remove the pan from the heat and stir in the vinegar.

When the potatoes are tender, transfer them to a serving dish. Toss them lightly with the bacon-fat mixture, dust with the chopped bacon, and season to taste with salt and pepper. Sprinkle with parsley and serve.

*Although the fashion is to leave new potatoes unpeeled in most recipes, in this one it is better to peel them because the skins begin to fall off after they have been cooked, and the result is not as attractive.*

*While bacon is by and large reserved for special occasions these days, its smoky flavor nicely complements the fish stew. Two tablespoons of olive oil can be substituted however.*

## BASQUE-STYLE FISH

*Serves 4*

While consulting the new edition of Larousse Gastronomique, *I came upon a recipe for a Basque fish stew called* ttoro *or* tioro. *Not only is the name unusual but so is the preparation. The fish is quickly seared in olive oil, placed in a plate, and then covered with a hot, well-seasoned fish broth to finish the cooking. This is my interpretation. Use the broth from the mussel recipe or a flavorful fish stock.*

¼ cup extra-virgin olive oil
1 medium onion, finely minced
¼ fresh fennel bulb, finely minced
1 medium red bell pepper, cored, seeded, and minced
2 garlic cloves, minced
1 medium, ripe tomato, cored and minced
¼ teaspoon hot red pepper flakes
Pinch of powdered saffron
½ cup dry white wine
1½ cups mussel broth or well-flavored fish stock
Salt and freshly ground black pepper
1 tablespoon fresh lemon juice
4 halibut steaks, 8 ounces each and about 1 inch thick; or 1¾ pounds thick tilefish fillets
⅓ cup all-purpose flour
2 tablespoons finely minced fresh parsley

Heat 2 tablespoons of the oil in a heavy saucepan. Add the onion, fennel, and bell pepper and cook over medium-low heat for about 10 minutes, or until the vegetables are soft but not brown. Stir in the garlic, tomato, red pepper flakes, and saffron and cook about 5 minutes longer. Add the wine and stock, bring to a simmer, and cook, partially covered, for about 5 minutes. Season to taste with salt, pepper, and lemon juice. Set aside.

A few minutes before serving, pat the fish dry with paper towels and dust them with flour. Heat the remaining oil in a large skillet over medium-high heat. Sear the fish until they are golden brown on both sides but not yet completely cooked through, about 3 minutes per side. Place a portion of fish in each of 4 shallow soup plates.

Reheat the broth to boiling. Spoon the hot stock with vegetables over each portion of fish, sprinkle with parsley, and serve with new potatoes.

*Basque-style fish, a lightly peppered regional stew, is served with steamed new potatoes.*

## BITTER CHOCOLATE CREAM WITH RASPBERRIES

*This chocolate cream is offered instead of chocolate truffles at the end of a dinner at Michel Bras's restaurant in France, where it is served in demitasse cups. But scooped onto a plate like ice cream and surrounded by raspberries, it is not just a little extra treat; it becomes an irresistibly delectable dessert.*

*Serves 4 to 6*

3 tablespoons slivered blanched almonds
¼ cup sugar
3 tablespoons plus ⅓ cup water
⅔ cup heavy cream
6 tablespoons (¾ stick) unsalted butter
¼ cup Dutch-processed cocoa
2 ounces bittersweet couverture chocolate, such as Callebaut, in small pieces
½ pint fresh raspberries
¾ cup heavy cream, whipped

Toast the almonds in a toaster oven or in a dry skillet, stirring them from time to time, until golden brown, about 5 minutes. Set aside.

Combine the sugar and 3 tablespoons water in a heavy, shallow pan. Cook without stirring over medium heat until the sugar turns amber, about 6 minutes. Stir in the toasted almonds, then immediately pour out the mixture onto a baking sheet or marble slab. Allow this praline to cool for 10 to 15 minutes, until it hardens.

Pulverize the cooled praline in a food processor until it is a fine powder, then transfer to a heavy saucepan. Add the cream, butter, and remaining ⅓ cup water. Cook over low heat until the butter and praline mixture have melted. Transfer the hot mixture to a food processor and process until the ingredients are just blended, then add the cocoa and chocolate and process until smooth. Transfer to a bowl. Chill at least 6 hours or overnight.

To serve, form oval scoops of the chocolate mixture with a tablespoon dipped in cold water, and place on chilled plates. Garnish each serving with some raspberries and whipped cream.

# HEARTY ITALIAN FARE

MOUSSE OF SALT COD
WILTED KALE
VEAL SHANKS EN CARBONNADE
SOFT POLENTA
FIG CAKE SPICED WITH CARDAMOM

◆

Despite its variety of seasonings, this cold-weather menu has a decidedly Italian cast. It might seem that the mousse of salt cod, most often associated with southern France, Spain, and Portugal, is out of place, but actually it is served in Italy, especially in the north. The veal, the same cut used for osso buco, is stewed with beer and onions the way a carbonnade would be prepared in Belgium. But by substituting veal shanks for the beef and serving them with a simple, creamy polenta, a Belgian recipe suits an Italian menu. To accompany this lusty veal dish I opt for wilted kale over the more typical broccoli rabe or escarole. The cake, derived from an ancient Byzantine recipe, suits a menu that suggests Italy.

As with many of the other menus for entertaining, this one lends itself to advance preparation and convenient reheating. With a salad garnish the mousse of salt cod is suitable as a plated first course, but it could also be served with drinks, with toast and oil-cured olives. The polenta should be made and kept warm just before the dinner is served. The kale requires only a last-minute stir-fry.

A well-structured wine from the Piedmont, such as Barolo, Barbaresco, or barbera d'Asti, would best complement the menu. And if you have a bottle of sweet fortified Italian wine such as Marsala or Malvasia on hand, it would be excellent with the cake. Strong yet syrupy vin santo would be another good choice.

## MOUSSE OF SALT COD

*The time it takes to soak salt cod to remove the salt is worth the effort because both its flavor and texture are unique. Pressed for time? Substitute a relatively nonoily smoked fish such as sturgeon or kippered salmon.*

*Serves 6*

1 pound salt cod
¾ cup extra-virgin olive oil
¾ to 1 cup milk, at room temperature
1 large garlic clove, finely chopped (or to taste)
Toasted French bread

Soak the salt cod for 24 to 48 hours in cold water, changing the water several times.

Once you are satisfied the fish is sufficiently desalinated and has softened, pick out any bones, break the fish into chunks, and place it in a saucepan. Cover the fish with water, bring to a boil, and simmer for 5 minutes; drain.

Grind the fish in a food processor. With the machine running, slowly add the olive oil, milk, and garlic and process until the mixture is light and fluffy, to the consistency of mashed potatoes.

Serve the mousse while it is still warm, as a dip or a first course with toast. The mousse can be made in advance and gently rewarmed in the top of a double-boiler before serving.

## WILTED KALE

*Kale has a wonderful, slightly chewy texture and a rich forest-green color. But once it has been cooked, especially with a splash of lemon added, it must be served at once or its green will begin to turn yellow.*

*Serves 6*

1 large bunch kale
2 tablespoons unsalted butter
2 garlic cloves, minced
2 scallions, minced
Juice of 1 lemon
Salt and freshly ground black pepper

Rinse and drain the kale; chop it coarsely.

Melt the butter in a large, heavy skillet over medium heat, then add the garlic and sauté it for a few seconds. Then add the kale and scallions. Increase heat to medium-high and stir-fry the kale until it has just wilted, about 5 minutes.

Stir in the lemon and season to taste with salt and pepper. Serve at once.

*Veal shanks en carbonnade, soft polenta, and wilted kale— substantial fare for fall*

## VEAL SHANKS EN CARBONNADE

*The shank of veal is a cut rich in natural gelatin, making it perfect for slow cooking with a resulting rich sauce. The bone is prized for its marrow, which is delicious (but not suitable for those on a low-fat diet; fortunately, there's only a mouthful or two). When buying veal shanks be sure they are single-serving size—about ¾ pound each.*

*This recipe combines the veal shanks with onions and beer, and it even works with other meats, like chicken drumsticks.*

*Serves 6*

2 tablespoons unsalted butter
2 tablespoons extra-virgin olive oil
6 cups very thinly sliced onions
4 large garlic cloves
6 pieces of veal shank, cut about 2 inches thick, about 4 to 4½ pounds
½ cup regular or amber beer
2 bay leaves
6 whole cloves
2 tablespoons balsamic vinegar
1 tablespoon Dijon mustard
Salt and freshly ground black pepper
2 tablespoons chopped fresh parsley

Melt the butter in a heatproof casserole large enough to hold the veal shanks snugly. Stir in the oil, then the onions. Cover and cook over medium-low heat until the onions are tender, about 15 minutes. Add the garlic and continue to cook, uncovered, stirring from time to time until the onions are golden, about 20 minutes. Remove the onions and garlic from the casserole, and reserve.

Dry the veal shanks. Place them in the casserole and brown them on both sides over medium heat. (You may not be able to do all of them at once.) When they are brown, remove them from the casserole and set aside.

Preheat the oven to 350°F.

Stir the beer into the casserole and bring to a simmer, scraping the bottom well. Add the bay leaves and cloves. Return the onions and garlic to the casserole, then add the veal shanks. Bring to a simmer, cover, and place in the oven. Cook for 2½ hours, turning the meat once or twice during the cooking, until it is very tender.

Carefully remove the meat from the casserole, place in a dish, and cover to keep warm. The sauce should have cooked down considerably. Stir in the vinegar and mustard. Season to taste with salt and pepper. Bring to a simmer.

Arrange the veal shanks on a platter and moisten with the sauce, pouring any remaining sauce around the shanks. Sprinkle with parsley and serve.

## SOFT POLENTA

*Serves 6*

1 tablespoon extra-virgin olive oil
1 large onion, finely chopped
5 cups well-seasoned chicken stock
1 cup yellow cornmeal, preferably stone-ground
3 tablespoons chopped fresh Italian parsley
¼ cup freshly grated Parmesan cheese (optional)

Heat the oil in a large, heavy saucepan over medium heat. Add the onion and sauté until it barely begins to brown, about 8 minutes. Add the chicken stock and bring to a simmer.

Pour the cornmeal very slowly into the simmering stock in a slow, thin, steady stream, stirring all the while. Do this is by taking handfuls of the cornmeal and allowing it to stream into the pot from a slightly open fist.

Continue cooking the polenta for 15 minutes, stirring from time to time. Transfer the polenta to a warm serving dish and sprinkle with parsley and cheese if desired. Serve at once.

**Note:** The polenta can be held for about 15 minutes by covering it with a piece of plastic wrap placed directly on the surface. Do not add the parsley and cheese until after removing the plastic at serving time. It can also be reheated in a microwave oven.

*P*olenta is a cornmeal-mush dish that is popular in northern Italy. It can be spooned onto a plate soft and warm, as in this recipe (the better to sop up a gravy), or it can be spread to cool, cut into squares, and grilled or fried, as Robert has done on page 179. Either way, it's home cooking at its best.

## FIG CAKE SPICED WITH CARDAMOM

*This recipe is adapted from one that is supposed to have been popular during the Byzantine Empire. It is easy to prepare and a lovely change of pace from raisin cake. It is excellent with coffee, especially cups of dark espresso or sweet Turkish coffee.*

*Serves 8*

1½ cups chopped dried brown figs
½ cup Port
1½ cups cake flour
1 teaspoon ground cardamom
1 teaspoon baking powder
¼ teaspoon baking soda
½ teaspoon salt
½ cup (1 stick) unsalted butter, softened
½ cup honey
2 large eggs
½ cup water

Preheat the oven to 350°F. Butter and flour an 8- or 9-inch springform pan.

Place the figs in a small bowl and mix with the wine. Set aside. Sift together the flour, cardamom, baking powder, baking soda, and salt. Set aside.

Beat the butter until fluffy. Slowly beat in the honey. Beat in the eggs one at a time and continue beating for about 1 minute.

Stir in the flour mixture in thirds, alternating with the water. Fold in the figs and wine. Spread the mixture in the prepared pan and bake about 55 minutes, or until a cake tester comes out clean.

# *ITALIAN FLAVORS FOR EARLY AUTUMN*

PLUM TOMATO SALAD WITH BASIL
VEAL SCALLOPINI WITH FRESH FIGS
RISOTTO WITH WILD RICE
WARM ITALIAN CHOCOLATE TORTE

◆

Clearly an autumn menu with its fresh figs, substantial risotto, and rich chocolate cake, this combination of dishes is one that guests find especially appealing. There is originality at work in this menu, but it is presented in a familiar framework.

For example, the last ripe plum tomatoes and verdant basil that linger from summer into fall are made into an appealing salad rather than the more expected pasta sauce. Pairing veal with fresh figs instead of the more typical mushrooms is particularly felicitous, as is adding some dark, earthy wild rice to a classic risotto. Even the chocolate cake is a bit out of the ordinary because it is served while still warm, which enhances its awesome intensity.

To prepare this menu, tackle the salad first, then the wild rice for the risotto. The remaining preparation of the risotto can be accomplished just before guests are seated, and the dish can be kept warm until you are ready to serve. The veal calls for a brief last-minute sauté after the first course has been cleared, and the cake should go into the oven about 45 minutes before the dinner is served.

A rich, well-structured Italian red wine, such as Brunello di Montalcino, Vino Nobile di Montepulciano, or one of the new sangiovese–cabernet sauvignon blends from Tuscany, would be my choice with this menu.

## PLUM TOMATO SALAD WITH BASIL

*Serves 4*

1 pound ripe plum tomatoes
2 tablespoons extra-virgin olive oil
2 tablespoons white wine vinegar
¼ cup fresh basil leaves, shredded
Salt and freshly ground black pepper

*Oval plum tomatoes are meatier than regular tomatoes and I rely on them for salads when regular tomatoes do not measure up to my standards. Leave underripe tomatoes in a basket on your kitchen counter; in a few days they will turn scarlet, tender, and lush.*

Quarter the tomatoes lengthwise and place in a bowl. Mix the olive oil and vinegar and pour over the tomatoes. Add the basil leaves and toss. Season to taste with salt and pepper and serve.

## VEAL SCALLOPINI WITH FRESH FIGS

*Serves 4*

1⅓ pounds veal scallopini, pounded thin
3 tablespoons flour
1 tablespoon unsalted butter
1 tablespoon extra-virgin olive oil
Salt and freshly ground black pepper
½ cup dry Marsala wine
6 fresh black figs, sliced
Few drops lemon juice

*Fresh figs—purple, green, or black—are in season during the summer and fall. They are exquisitely succulent, and they are especially well complemented by Marsala wine. Look for figs that yield to the touch but have no soft spots or bruises.*

Pat the veal dry with paper towels and dust lightly with flour.

Heat the butter and oil in one or two large skillets. Add the veal and sauté over high heat until lightly browned, about 2 minutes on each side. Transfer veal to a warm serving platter and season with salt and pepper.

Add the Marsala to the pan and cook over medium heat, scraping the pan, until the wine has reduced by half. (If you used 2 pans for cooking the veal, use only one of them for making the sauce.) Add the figs and cook, stirring gently, a minute or so longer, until the figs are warmed through but still hold their shape. Stir in the lemon juice. Pour the sauce over the veal and serve at once.

## RISOTTO WITH WILD RICE

*Serves 4*

**4 cups hot beef or chicken stock**
**½ cup wild rice, rinsed**
**2 tablespoons unsalted butter or olive oil**
**½ cup finely chopped onion**
**1 cup Italian Arborio rice**
**Salt and freshly ground black pepper to taste**

Bring 1¼ cups of the stock to a boil in a small saucepan, add the wild rice, cover, and cook until the rice is tender and nearly all the liquid has been absorbed, about 45 minutes.

While the wild rice is cooking, heat the butter or oil in a large, heavy saucepan. Add the onion and cook slowly until very tender but not brown, about 8 minutes. Add the Arborio rice and stir well.

Begin adding the remaining hot stock, ½ cup at a time, stirring constantly and adding more stock as each portion is absorbed by the rice. After 20 to 25 minutes all the stock should have been added and the rice should be just tender. Remove from heat.

When the wild rice has finished cooking, fold it and any remaining liquid into the risotto. Gently reheat the risotto if necessary, season to taste, and serve.

*Since risotto came into fashion I have seen recipes for "risottos" made with everything under the sun—even potatoes and barley. But the name risotto connotes a specific way of preparing a particular kind of rice with broth.*

*In this risotto, prepared according to the most basic Italian recipe, the flavor is varied by the last-minute addition of wild rice. Unlike the short-grained Arborio rice, wild rice, like other long-grained rices, cannot be cooked with the risotto method. The grains crumble and fall apart.*

## WARM ITALIAN CHOCOLATE TORTE

*Serves 6 to 8*

8 ounces pine nuts (about 1 cup)
1 cup granulated sugar
1 cup (2 sticks) unsalted butter, softened
4 large eggs, separated
¾ cup Dutch-processed cocoa
1 teaspoon instant coffee
   Confectioners' sugar
1 cup heavy cream, whipped

*This is the irresistibly intense chocolate torte that Sandro Fioriti, a jolly bear of a chef, serves warm in his restaurant, Sandro's, in New York.*

*Although the cake is most delicious served while still warm, it can be made in advance and served cooled to room temperature if that is more convenient.*

Line the bottom of an 8-inch springform cake pan with wax paper, butter the paper and the sides of the pan, and dust with flour. Preheat the oven to 350°F.

Combine the nuts with ¼ cup of the granulated sugar in a food processor and process just until the nuts are finely ground; don't let them turn into a paste. Remove the nut mixture from the food processor and set aside.

Place the butter and the remaining granulated sugar in the food processor and process until well blended and fluffy. Add the egg yolks one at a time and process for 30 seconds after each addition. Transfer this mixture to a bowl. Mix the cocoa with the ground nuts, then fold them into the butter mixture. Stir in the instant coffee.

Beat the egg whites until they hold peaks but are still creamy-textured and not dry. Fold them into the chocolate batter, spread the batter in the cake pan, and bake until the top of the cake is firm to the touch and a cake tester comes out clean, about 50 minutes.

Allow the cake to cool in the pan on a rack for 15 minutes, then remove the sides of the pan and continue cooling the cake for 45 minutes to 1 hour longer. Invert the cake onto a plate, remove the bottom of the pan, and peel off the paper. Reinvert cake onto a serving dish. Dust the top of the cake heavily with sifted confectioners' sugar and serve at once, while still warm, with whipped cream.

*Intense, rich Italian chocolate torte served warm*

# A Menu for All Seasons

Leeks and Fennel in Anise Vinaigrette
Coq au Vin with Shiitake Mushrooms
Potato Pasta
Classic Caramel Custard

◆

This dinner clearly illustrates how menus for entertaining can evolve from routine family meals. Some small touches are all it takes to make everyday food special.

The coq au vin is a good example. A relatively straightforward chicken stew, here it is made with dried shiitake mushrooms to add more intense flavor. The potato pasta, one of the first recipes my mother taught me, is only a trifle more elaborate than good mashed potatoes.

Were it a menu for family, however, a simple dish of leeks vinaigrette would have sufficed as a first course. Combining the leeks with fennel gives the dish an innovative cast, and guests always find it appealing. The caramel custard is one of my very favorite dishes, something I adore sharing with friends.

The entire menu is excellent for entertaining because every dish (up to the actual boiling of the pasta) can be prepared as much as two days in advance. The menu is also an easy one to increase to serve six or eight.

For guests I see this as a two-wine dinner, beginning with a crisp white wine, like a Sancerre from the Loire, followed by an unpretentious red wine, such as a lesser château-bottled Bordeaux, a California cabernet sauvignon, or a blend of cabernet sauvignon and shiraz from Australia.

## LEEKS AND FENNEL IN ANISE VINAIGRETTE

*Serves 4*

4 medium leeks
1 large fennel bulb
8 cups water
½ cup tarragon vinegar
   Salt
1 garlic clove
1 tablespoon fresh tarragon leaves
1 teaspoon anise seed
¼ cup extra-virgin olive oil

Trim the leeks so there is only about 1 inch of green. Slit them vertically about two-thirds of the way down from the top, slice off the roots, and wash them well.

Rinse the fennel and cut off the stems, reserving a large bunch of the leaves. Trim the root end flush with the bulb and pare off any brown spots. Slice the bulb vertically into 4 sections, each about 1 inch thick.

Bring the water and ¼ cup of the vinegar to a simmer in a pan large enough to hold the leeks and the fennel pieces in a single layer. Add the fennel leaves and a generous pinch of salt, and simmer 15 minutes. Add the leeks and fennel, cover, and poach gently 15 to 20 minutes, or until the vegetables are tender. Remove the leeks and fennel pieces from the pan and set them on several thicknesses of paper towel to drain thoroughly, turning them once. Discard the fennel leaves.

Meanwhile, grind the garlic, tarragon leaves, and anise seed together in a spice grinder, blender, or mortar. Mix with the remaining vinegar and beat in the olive oil. Season the dressing with salt.

When the leeks and fennel are thoroughly drained, arrange them in a serving dish. Beat the dressing again and pour it evenly over the vegetables. Allow to marinate at room temperature at least 1 hour before serving.

*P*oached leeks served cold in a vinaigrette sauce are traditional in French homes and bistros. This variation combines leeks with the anise flavor of fennel in a vinaigrette that is lightly seasoned with crushed anise seed, subtly underscoring the note of licorice contributed by the fennel. One advantage of this recipe is that if one of the main ingredients—the leeks or the fennel—is not available, the dish can be made with just the other.

## COQ AU VIN WITH SHIITAKE MUSHROOMS

*One winter weekend at a friend's country house I decided to prepare coq au vin for dinner. The hostess could not find fresh mushrooms at the local store, but she happened to have some dried Chinese black mushrooms, shiitakes, on hand. We used them, with excellent results. They have a richer, earthier flavor than plain fresh cultivated mushrooms and a meatier texture as well. The soaking liquid also deepens the flavor of the sauce.*

*Serves 4*

1 ounce dried shiitake or Chinese black mushrooms
1 cup warm water
1 ounce slab bacon, finely diced
1 tablespoon vegetable oil
1 frying chicken, about 3½ pounds, cut up, with skin removed if desired
6 ounces small white onions, peeled
¼ cup finely chopped carrot
2 tablespoons finely minced shallots
¼ cup finely chopped onion
1 tablespoon flour
1½ cups dry red wine
Salt and freshly ground black pepper
½ teaspoon dried thyme
2 tablespoons Cognac or brandy
1 tablespoon finely chopped fresh parsley

Place the mushrooms in a bowl, cover with the warm water, and allow to soak 30 to 40 minutes, until softened.

Meanwhile, in a heavy casserole sauté the bacon in the oil until golden and crisp. Remove the bacon bits from the pan with a slotted spoon and reserve. Add the chicken pieces to the fat in the skillet and brown over high heat. You may have to do this in several batches. Remove the chicken from the pan.

Toss the white onions in the hot pan for about 5 minutes, or until lightly browned. Remove the onions from the pan and reserve, then lower the heat. Add the carrot, shallots, and chopped onion, and sauté until tender, about 5 minutes. Stir in the flour, then whisk in the wine. Bring to a simmer and season lightly with salt and pepper. Add the thyme and return the chicken and bacon to the casserole.

*The classic coq au vin updated with shiitake mushrooms*

Drain the mushrooms, reserving the liquid. Remove and discard any tough stems. Add the mushrooms to the casserole along with the soaking liquid.

Cover the casserole and simmer over low heat for 30 minutes. Add the white onions and cook about 20 minutes longer, until the onions are tender and the chicken is done. Stir in the Cognac or brandy, and serve sprinkled with the parsley.

## POTATO PASTA

*Serves 4*

1 **large baking potato, peeled and cut into chunks**
1 **large egg, lightly beaten**
1 **teaspoon salt, or to taste**
²⁄₃ **to ¾ cup all-purpose flour**
2 **tablespoons unsalted butter**
¼ **cup dry bread crumbs**

*Long before I knew what gnocchi were I remember my mother making these fat little noodle shapes with a mashed potato dough. They have always been a favorite. They also can be served as a separate course with a tomato sauce, or the dough can be seasoned with minced herbs.*

Boil the potato until it is tender, about 20 minutes. Finely mash it and allow to cool to lukewarm. Stir in the egg and salt. Mix in enough flour to make a soft dough that is not sticky.

Transfer the dough to a floured board and knead lightly for a minute or two. Roll or pat into a rectangle about 8 × 12 inches and ¼ inch thick. Cut the dough into strips ¼ inch wide and cut the strips into 1-inch pieces.

Melt the butter in a small skillet. Add the bread crumbs and toss in the butter for 2 to 3 minutes, until warmed and lightly browned. Set aside. Bring a kettle of salted water to a boil, drop in the pasta, and boil about 3 minutes, until they rise to the surface. Drain thoroughly, then toss gently with buttered bread crumbs.

## CLASSIC CARAMEL CUSTARD

*Serves 4*

1 cup sugar
3 tablespoons water
3 large eggs
2 large egg yolks
2½ cups milk
½ cup heavy cream
1 teaspoon vanilla extract

Preheat the oven to 350°F.

Swirl ½ cup of the sugar with the water in a 2-quart saucepan, preferably nonstick, and cook without stirring over medium-high heat until the mixture turns amber, about 6 minutes. Remove from heat, pour into a 4-cup baking dish, and tilt the dish to coat the bottom with the caramel.

In a medium bowl, beat the eggs and egg yolks together. Beat in the remaining ½ cup sugar and stir in the milk, cream, and vanilla. Pour into the baking dish.

Set the dish in a pan of hot water that comes about halfway up the sides of the dish. Place in the oven and bake for 45 minutes, or until a knife inserted in the center comes out clean.

Allow the custard to cool to room temperature, then refrigerate it for 6 hours or overnight. To unmold, run a knife around the edges and invert onto a serving dish with enough of a rim to catch the liquid caramel.

*The trickiest part of making caramel custard is preparing the caramel. When sugar is cooked (with a little water to dissolve it), it goes through a series of stages as the temperature increases. Caramelization begins to take place at around 310°F. At around 345°F. the caramelization is complete and the caramel mixture should be removed from the heat and used at once, while it is still fluid. Never taste or touch caramel before it has cooled because it is scorchingly hot.*

*One final tip: Maida Heatter, the author of so many wonderful dessert books, recommends caramelizing in a nonstick pan so none of the mixture is left in the pan. It also makes clean-ups easier.*

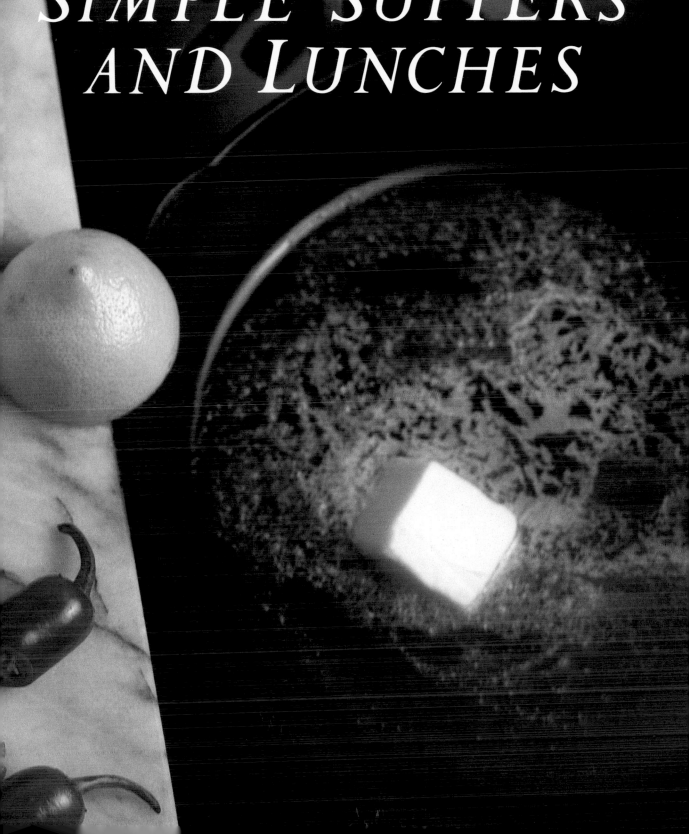

# SIMPLE SUPPERS
# AND LUNCHES

*T*he gracious informality that has become so welcome at home allows a host or hostess to entertain by improvising, to invite friends for lunch or supper on the spur of the moment. A gathering for lunch on a summer weekend does not require elaborate planning, and a spontaneous supper at home after a movie or a sporting event is not just possible, it is an enjoyable alternative to a restaurant for all involved.

The menus for these occasions generally are simpler than dinners, with less lavish desserts and more basic wines. They almost always consist of fewer courses. Sometimes a big pot of homey soup, rounded out with good bread and an attractive salad, is all it takes. The soup might even come out of freezer containers, reheated in a generous saucepan or, more rapidly, in a microwave oven. Or a substantial salad might serve as the meal's anchor.

Occasionally the inspiration is some especially felicitous assemblage of leftovers, refined and turned into a midday meal for guests. I have found that virtually anything can become a good pasta sauce, a salad, or a soup.

In summer a quick run to the farm stand or the fish market can yield the makings of a fabulous lunch. When I bring home half a dozen excellent tomatoes, some tiny potatoes, perfect strawberries, or plump scallops, I'd rather not wait until dinner to share and enjoy them.

Some of these relatively no-frills menus require minimal time in the supermarket or in the kitchen. Few call for forays into specialty food shops. In fact, a couple of them can be assembled from staples on the pantry shelf and in the refrigerator without compromising taste and flair. The Whole Wheat Pecan Cake (page 115) is one irresistible example; the Pappa al Pomodoro (page 118) is another.

In other sections of this book you will find many recipes that can be adapted for lunches or quick suppers. When doubled, some of the more substantial first courses, with a salad and some interesting bread, easily become luncheon main dishes. You might try the Herbed Mussels (page 66) or the Smokey Risotto (page 34).

# MY FAVORITE LUNCH

## CLAMS AND TOMATOES WITH LINGUINE
## CHOPPED SALAD
## PARMESAN CHEESE AND GRAPES

◆

This menu does double duty. It provides a quick and enjoyable light supper almost any time, and on weekends in summer it often becomes lunch. It's excellent as a menu for guests or for family. Either way it requires a scant half-hour to put together. The most time-consuming step is waiting for the water to boil for the linguine.

The first-course salad is primarily a marketing effort: selecting an assortment of vegetables that are in good condition. Preparation can be simplified with the substitution of a good, basic green salad made with leaf lettuce, Boston, or Bibb. Similarly, the fruit can be varied according to what the market has on hand. Fresh figs or pears are two tempting alternatives.

Select a sauvignon blanc or a light red wine, served cool, to accompany the meal.

*Parmesan cheese to nibble with grapes*

## CLAMS AND TOMATOES
## WITH LINGUINE

*Serves 4*

3 tablespoons extra-virgin olive oil
3 garlic cloves, chopped
¼ cup chopped onion
36 littleneck clams, scrubbed
1 cup chopped fresh plum tomatoes
½ cup dry white wine
1 pound linguine
　Generous pinch of dried hot red pepper flakes
1 tablespoon chopped fresh Italian parsley
1 tablespoon finely shredded fresh basil leaves

*T*wo types of clams are acceptable for this recipe: either the small, hard clams called littlenecks, or the new cultivated Manila clams, which are even smaller, have oval shells with ombre striping, and are thoroughly delicious.

Use dried linguine, not fresh. Also, do not add grated cheese. In Italy, grated cheese is never served with seafood pasta, and with good reason: it distorts the naturally briny flavor of the dish. Instead, save the cheese for dessert.

Bring a large pot of salted water to a boil for the linguine.

Heat the oil in a heavy saucepan. Add the garlic and onion, and sauté over low heat about 5 minutes.

Stir in the clams, then stir in the tomatoes and wine. Cover the pan and cook over medium-low heat until the clams have opened, about 10 minutes.

While the clams are cooking, boil the linguine until al dente, about 7 minutes. Drain and divide onto 4 warm plates.

Season the clams and sauce with pepper flakes. Taste the sauce to be sure it is not too salty, and add a little water to cut the saltiness if necessary. Spoon the clams in their shells and the sauce over the linguine. Sprinkle each serving with parsley and basil, and serve at once.

## CHOPPED SALAD

### Serves 4

1 medium, ripe tomato, diced
½ medium cucumber, peeled, seeded, and diced
½ cup chopped fennel bulb
⅓ cup chopped red bell pepper
6 red radishes, diced
2 scallions, diced
2 tablespoons white wine vinegar
2 tablespoons extra-virgin olive oil
Salt and freshly ground black pepper
Pinch of cayenne pepper

*This type of salad, almost a slaw, is extremely versatile. It is a kitchen-sink mixture that can be varied according to what looks fresh in the market and what is on hand in the refrigerator.*

Combine the tomato, cucumber, fennel, red pepper, radishes, and scallions in a large bowl.

Mix the vinegar and oil, pour over the salad, and toss. Season with the salt, black pepper, and cayenne pepper.

## PARMESAN CHEESE AND GRAPES

### Serves 4

8 to 10 ounces Parmigiano-Reggiano or Grana cheese
1 large bunch grapes

*Even for grating over pasta, it is worth buying the best Parmesan cheese. Its distinctive flavor makes all the difference. Genuine Parmigiano-Reggiano from Italy has a nutty sharpness, a slightly crunchy texture, and a complexity the others lack. Always check the rind, which is stamped with the name.*

Break the cheese into 4 portions using the point of a knife or a Parmesan cheese server, a small pointed utensil used to chisel small fragments from a large wedge. Snip the grapes into 4 or 8 small clusters.

Divide the cheese and grapes among 4 plates and serve. In Italy the small bits of cheese are eaten without benefit of fork and knife, but you may prefer to offer them if the blocks of cheese are too large to eat in a bite or two.

# A FRESH FISH LUNCH

## PAN-FRIED WHITING
## WITH JALAPEÑO MAYONNAISE
## PARSLIED SQUASH
## CHERRY-CARDAMOM RICE PUDDING

◆

I love finding small, superbly fresh whole fish in a market, tossing them in cornmeal, and briefly pan-frying them, campfire style. It's the kind of dish that is most suitable as a lunch for two, because the frying can all be accomplished at once and the fish served hot and lightly crisped from the pan. For a substantial Sunday brunch I scramble some eggs to serve on the side.

First, ready the rice pudding for dessert, then tackle the squash. The final step before frying the fish is to prepare the mayonnaise.

Beer or everyday white wine are my beverage choices for this menu.

*Fresh whiting rolled in cornmeal sizzling in the skillet*

## PAN-FRIED WHITING

*Serves 2*

2 whole whiting, cleaned, about 2½ pounds
2 garlic cloves, lightly mashed
  Salt and freshly ground black pepper
¼ cup all-purpose flour
¼ cup white cornmeal
½ cup milk
2 tablespoons unsalted butter
  Lemon wedges and parsley, for garnish

*Small whole whiting are perfect for this recipe. Smelts (three to four per serving, depending on size), whole trout, butterfish, or small "tinker" mackerel are suitable substitutes. Fish fillets (catfish, flounder) can also be used. With fillets, a pound of fish is ample for two.*

Rinse and dry the fish. Rub the fish inside and out with one garlic clove and season with salt and pepper.

Combine the flour and cornmeal. Season to taste with salt and pepper. Dip the fish in the milk, then roll in the cornmeal mixture.

In a large, heavy skillet, melt the butter over medium-high heat. Add the garlic to the melting butter, then remove it before it has a chance to brown. Add the fish to the pan and sauté until golden brown, about 3 to 5 minutes on each side.

Transfer the fish to a serving platter, garnish with the lemon and parsley, and serve with Jalapeño Mayonnaise.

## JALAPEÑO MAYONNAISE

*Makes ⅓ cup*

3 tablespoons mayonnaise
1 tablespoon plain yogurt
1 jalapeño pepper, seeded and finely diced
1 scallion, trimmed and minced
½ tablespoon ground cumin
1 tablespoon minced fresh coriander

*Fresh jalapeño peppers are first choice for this spicy condiment, but other fresh green chilies or even canned chilies can stand in if necessary.*

Mix the mayonnaise and yogurt in a bowl. Add the remaining ingredients and stir well.

## PARSLIED SQUASH

*Serves 2*

1½ pounds winter squash, such as acorn, butternut, calabaza, or pumpkin
1 teaspoon finely minced garlic
Salt and freshly ground black pepper
2 tablespoons extra-virgin olive oil
½ cup finely chopped Italian parsley

Preheat the oven to 425°F.

Pare off the skin of the squash using a very sharp knife. Cut the squash in half and scoop out the seeds and strings. Dice the flesh into 1-inch cubes.

Place the cubes in a shallow baking dish and toss with the remaining ingredients. Bake about 25 minutes, tossing once or twice during the baking, until the squash is tender.

*In France and Italy, hard-skinned winter squash and pumpkin are combined with garlic and olive oil, giving them irresistible character and flavor quite unlike the sweet and spiced style of preparation usually served here. This recipe is my version.*

## CHERRY-CARDAMOM RICE PUDDING

*Serves 2*

⅓ cup long-grain rice
¼ cup sugar
½ teaspoon ground cardamom
2 cups milk
⅓ cup dried sour cherries
2 small scoops vanilla ice cream (optional)

Combine all the ingredients except the ice cream in a heavy saucepan. Bring to a boil, then lower heat to a gentle simmer. Cook covered, stirring from time to time, until the rice is very tender, about 40 minutes.

Divide between two dishes and refrigerate until ready to serve. Top with a small scoop of vanilla ice cream, if desired.

*Rice puddings can be humble, comforting desserts, rich with the memories of childhood. This may be the simplest way to make a good, thick, tender rice pudding. Seasoning the pudding with cardamom and replacing the traditional raisins with dried sour cherries are touches that reflect today's cooking.*

# A WARM AND COMFORTING SUPPER

WALNUT AND ROQUEFORT SALAD

CHICKEN IN THE POT

OLD-FASHIONED CHOCOLATE PUDDING WITH
CINNAMON CREAM

CHOCOLATE CHIP CRISPS

*Leftover Bonus:* CHICKEN SALAD WITH
FRESH CORIANDER

◆

Essentially a one-dish meal, chicken in the pot combines a restorative soup with moist pieces of chicken, vegetables, and homey noodles. It is always welcomed on a chilly day. Care should be taken in preparing the soup, but the extra effort pays off with invitingly clear, golden results.

A simple salad adorned with crumbled Roquefort cheese and toasted walnuts, and a comforting chocolate pudding made easily from scratch, round out this humble yet appealing menu. Guests adore being served chocolate pudding. To dress it up you may prefer to spoon it into stemmed goblets.

Any chicken that is left over can be put to dozens of uses. One of my favorites is a salad that sparks the fairly bland meat with some Southwestern spice.

Because the chicken is basically poached and served with broth, a white wine, notably a low-priced chardonnay from California or Australia, would be best with this menu.

*Old-fashioned chocolate pudding is tempting to taste right out of the saucepan.*

*I love tangy cheeses, especially the blue-veined variety, in salads. In my view, when they're crumbled over a vinaigrette rather than mixed into a dressing, their flavor has more impact.*

*Only the cheese made and aged in the caves of the French village of Roquefort-sous-Soulzon is entitled to be called Roquefort. This salad is served everywhere in that chilly, craggy region.*

## WALNUT AND ROQUEFORT SALAD

*Serves 4*

**3 tablespoons coarsely chopped walnuts**
**1 head Boston lettuce, or 2 to 3 heads Bibb lettuce, rinsed and dried**
**1 tablespoon white wine vinegar**
**3 tablespoons extra-virgin olive oil**
**¼ cup crumbled Roquefort cheese**
**Freshly ground black pepper**

Toast the walnuts in a toaster oven or in a dry skillet until lightly browned. Tear the lettuce into bite-size pieces and place in a salad bowl.

Beat the vinegar and oil together; pour over the salad and toss. Scatter the cheese and walnuts over the salad, season with pepper, and serve.

*There is an art to making chicken soup, and mastering it was the first serious cooking instruction I received from my mother. She always insisted that in addition to having a rich flavor and golden color, her chicken soup be clean as a whistle. She skimmed, skimmed, skimmed in the beginning, then strained the soup through a linen napkin. Preventing the soup from coming to a hard rolling boil after the initial skimming also keeps it clear.*

## CHICKEN IN THE POT

*Serves 4*

**1 chicken, about 3½ pounds, split**
**1 large onion, trimmed of roots but unpeeled**
**2 large carrots, peeled**
**2 celery stalks with leaves**
**2 garlic cloves, crushed**
**1 parsley sprig and 1 dill sprig, tied together**
**Salt**
**¼ pound narrow egg noodles**
**4 medium, firm white mushrooms, wiped clean**
**1 tablespoon finely minced fresh parsley**
**1 tablespoon finely minced fresh chives**

Pull off as much of the yellow fat as possible from the chicken. Place chicken halves in a 5- or 6-quart pot along with the gizzard, neck, and heart (reserve the liver for another purpose). Cover with cold water, bring to a boil, and boil gently for about 5 minutes, skimming off the foam and scum that accumulate on the surface.

Lower the heat to a simmer and add the onion, carrots, celery, garlic, and herbs. Stir in salt to taste—you may need as much as 1 tablespoon.

Simmer gently for 1 hour to 1 hour, 15 minutes, until the chicken is done. The thigh juices will run clear when the flesh is pricked. At no time should the liquid boil; this will cause the finished soup to be cloudy.

When the chicken is done, remove it from the pot and set it aside, covered, to keep warm. Strain the soup through a fine strainer or a strainer lined with a clean linen napkin, reserving the carrots, the onion, and one celery stalk. (Discard the remaining vegetables. Wash out the soup pot, and return the soup to the pot. The soup should be clear and golden with very little fat on the surface. (Chilling it overnight will allow you to remove all the fat, if you wish.)

Finely dice the reserved carrots and celery and the herbs. Remove the skin from the onion and dice half of the onion and reserve. Discard the remaining onion.

Boil the noodles in a separate pot of water until tender, then set aside, covered, to keep warm.

Remove the skin from the chicken and discard, then cut the chicken into serving pieces. Slice the mushrooms very thin.

To serve, reheat the soup to a simmer and return the chicken to the pot. Simmer for 5 minutes. Place a couple of pieces of chicken in each of 4 deep bowls along with some of the noodles and diced vegetables. Add some of the mushroom slices to each. Ladle hot soup over each serving. Sprinkle with parsley and chives and serve.

*When I want to make just chicken soup—to serve as a first course, for example—I do not use a whole chicken. I make the soup following this same recipe from the various backs, necks, wingtips, and gizzards stored in my freezer. But I never use the livers in soup because they would make the broth bitter. Freeze livers separately for another purpose. The excess fat removed from the whole chicken can also be frozen to use for cooking.*

## OLD-FASHIONED CHOCOLATE PUDDING WITH CINNAMON CREAM

*How simple it is to make pudding from scratch! You could even keep a canister of the dry ingredients, in the correct proportions, in the cupboard, like a homemade mix, so you'll never have to resort to the commercial variety.*

*Serves 4*

⅓ **cup cocoa**
⅓ **cup plus 2 tablespoons sugar**
4½ **tablespoons cornstarch**
2¼ **cups milk**
1 **teaspoon vanilla extract**
1 **teaspoon ground cinnamon**
⅔ **cup heavy cream, well chilled**

Using a whisk, mix the cocoa, ⅓ cup sugar, and the cornstarch in a heavy 2-quart saucepan. Gradually add the milk, whisking constantly, until the mixture is smooth.

Place the pan over medium heat and cook, whisking constantly, until the mixture just comes to a boil, has thickened, and is very smooth. Stir in the vanilla.

Transfer the pudding to individual dishes or goblets and place plastic wrap directly on the surface of the pudding to prevent a skin from forming.

Just before serving, mix the remaining 2 tablespoons sugar with the cinnamon and stir into the heavy cream. Whip the cream until it holds soft peaks. Serve the pudding warm or chilled, topped with the cream.

## CHOCOLATE CHIP CRISPS

*These chocolate chip crisps provide a crunchy textural contrast to the smooth pudding. If desired, some or all of the pecans and chocolate chips can be replaced with other nuts, rolled oats, currants, or raisins.*

*Makes about 4 dozen cookies*

2 **eggs**
1¼ **cups light brown sugar, packed**
1 **cup granulated sugar**
¾ **cup flour**
¼ **cup (½ stick) melted, unsalted butter**
1 **teaspoon vanilla extract**
1½ **cups finely chopped pecans**
1 **cup miniature chocolate chips**

Preheat the oven to 350°F. Butter and flour at least two large baking sheets.

Beat the eggs until very thick and light. Beat in the brown sugar, then the granulated sugar. Stir in the flour, melted butter, and vanilla, then fold in the pecans and chocolate chips.

Drop the cookies from a teaspoon onto the prepared baking sheets, leaving about 2 inches of space between them. Bake 12 to 15 minutes, until very lightly browned. Allow the cookies to cool on the baking sheets for at least 10 minutes before removing them with a spatula.

## *Leftover Bonus:*
## CHICKEN SALAD WITH FRESH CORIANDER

### *Serves 4*

1 tablespoon Dijon mustard
¼ cup sherry vinegar
⅓ cup extra-virgin olive oil
 Salt and freshly ground black pepper
1 red bell pepper, seeded, cored, and slivered
1 green bell pepper, seeded, cored, and slivered
½ red onion, sliced paper thin
1 tablespoon minced scallion
1 teaspoon minced fresh chili pepper
1½ cups diced cooked chicken
¼ cup fresh coriander leaves, coarsely chopped

Beat the mustard and vinegar together in a salad bowl. Beat in the olive oil. Season the dressing to taste.

Add the peppers, onion, scallion, and chili pepper, and mix. Add the chicken and toss all the ingredients together. Just before serving, fold in the coriander.

*One of the infinite varieties of chicken salad, this one is seasoned with peppers, chili powder, and coriander for a Southwestern approach. Serve it as an entrée salad or in a sandwich. It would even be delicious rolled inside flour tortillas and, wrapped in foil, warmed in the oven. When preparing the salad, the chicken will look better if you take the time to tear it into small pieces by hand rather than cutting it.*

# A SPRING LUNCH MENU

---

ROSEMARY FOCACCIA

FETTUCCINE WITH SMOKED SALMON
AND ASPARAGUS

TOASTED COCONUT MACAROONS

HONEYED STRAWBERRIES

---

◆

This light, springtime lunch begins with a fragrant focaccia, or pizza bread; then continues with a toss of noodles, smoked salmon, and seasonal asparagus; and ends with fresh strawberries, at their best from April through June.

The macaroons lend themselves to advance preparation, and the strawberries can be readied before guests arrive. The focaccia, however, is best if it's eaten shortly after emerging from the oven, and the pasta is a last-minute operation.

Select a crisp but full-bodied white wine such as a Chablis from France, an herbaceous sauvignon blanc from California, or a refreshing Italian white wine, like a Tuscan vernaccia di San Gimignano, to serve with this meal.

## ROSEMARY FOCACCIA

*Serves 3 to 4*

1 package active dry yeast
 Pinch of sugar
1 cup warm water (105°–115°F.)
 Salt
3 cups all-purpose flour (approximately)
1 tablespoon extra-virgin olive oil
1 teaspoon fresh or dried rosemary

Mix the yeast with the sugar in a large bowl and dissolve in about ¼ cup of the warm water. Set aside for about 5 minutes, until the yeast bubbles. Add the remaining water and ½ teaspoon of salt. Stir in 1 cup of the flour and blend well. Stir in 1 to 1½ cups more flour, ½ cup at a time, until a ball of dough can be formed. Sprinkle with some of the remaining flour and knead the dough right in the bowl for about 7 minutes, adding more flour as necessary to keep the dough from becoming too sticky.

Brush the top of the dough with a teaspoon or so of the oil, then turn it in the bowl and brush the other side. Cover and set aside to rise until doubled, about 1 hour.

Preheat the oven to 500°F. Lightly oil a 12- to 14-inch pizza pan.

Punch the dough down and roll or stretch it to fit the pan. Prick dough at 1-inch intervals to prevent it from rising. Brush it with the remaining oil, then sprinkle with the rosemary and additional salt. Place on the lowest rack in the oven and bake about 15 minutes, until browned. Cut into wedges or squares and serve while still warm.

*Focaccia consists of a basic dough rolled out and brushed with olive oil, dusted with herbs, or paved with thin slices of vegetable before baking. Plain focaccia can be baked, then returned to the oven with a topping of some sort, even cheese, to make an instant pizza. It can even be stuffed.*

*The name of this traditional, rustic food comes from the Latin* focus, *meaning "hearth" (ponder that connection a bit), but it varies regionally. In the area around Venice a sweet focaccia is called* fugassa; *in southern France, this becomes* fougasse, *while in the Loire Valley it's* fouace *or* fouasse.

# FETTUCCINE WITH SMOKED SALMON AND ASPARAGUS

*Delectable, attractive, and quick to prepare, this is a perfect springtime luncheon dish. Serve it as a first course at a dinner, followed by a simple main dish such as roast chicken.*

*Smoked salmon comes in many levels of quality at assorted prices. Use a good-quality salmon for this recipe: the salmon is barely cooked and the flavor should be delicate.*

*Serves 3 to 4*

½ pound fresh medium asparagus
1 tablespoon unsalted butter
½ tablespoon minced shallots
1 cup heavy cream
4 ounces smoked salmon, sliced ¼ inch thick
Freshly ground black pepper
1 teaspoon fresh lemon juice
9 to 10 ounces fresh green fettuccine noodles
2 tablespoons minced fresh dill

Snap off the ends of the asparagus where they break naturally. Cut the asparagus on a slant into pieces about 1 inch long.

Steam the asparagus until they are just barely tender and still bright green, about 3 minutes. Rinse under cold water, drain well on paper towels, and set aside.

Bring a large pot of water to a boil for the pasta.

While the water is coming to the boil, melt the butter in a large, heavy skillet. Add the shallots and sauté over low heat until soft but not brown, about 3 minutes. Stir in the cream and simmer about 5 minutes, until the cream has thickened somewhat.

Cut the salmon into slivers, add it to the cream, and remove the skillet from the heat. Season with pepper and lemon juice. Add the asparagus.

When the pot of water is boiling add the fettuccine. Stir once or twice, then cook 2 or 3 minutes after the water has returned to the boil. Drain well and transfer to a warm serving dish. Reheat the sauce, pour it over the fettuccine, and sprinkle with dill. Serve at once.

*A spring lunch features fettuccine with asparagus and slivers of smoked salmon.*

## TOASTED COCONUT MACAROONS

*Makes about 15 macaroons*

**1½ cups grated unsweetened coconut**
**2 large egg whites, at room temperature**
**Pinch of salt**
**⅔ cup sugar**

Preheat the broiler. Spread the coconut on a foil-lined baking sheet and place under the broiler. Toast it, watching it carefully and stirring it so it browns evenly, until the coconut is honey-colored, a minute or two.

Preheat the oven to 300°F. Grease and flour a large baking sheet.

Beat the egg whites with the salt until softly peaked. Gradually add the sugar and continue beating until stiff and glossy, about 5 minutes. Fold in the coconut.

On the baking sheet, shape the batter into 1½-inch mounds, leaving 1 inch between each. Place in the oven and bake for 30 to 40 minutes, until fairly firm.

Remove from the oven and allow to cool on the baking sheet.

*The grated coconut sold in supermarkets and grocery stores is sweetened—too much so. The unsweetened grated coconut (also called dessicated) that is available in health food stores is far preferable. Alternatively, you can start with a whole coconut, grate your own, and keep it stored in the freezer. Store macaroons in the freezer or in an airtight jar.*

## HONEYED STRAWBERRIES

*Serves 4*

**1½ pints fresh strawberries**
**3 tablespoons honey**
**2 tablespoons kirsch**

Rinse and hull the strawberries. Combine the honey and kirsch, pour over the berries, and macerate for 1 hour before serving.

*Although strawberries are in the market all year, they're best in spring and early summer, from April through June. Look for berries that are uniformly red, with no soft spots, and capped with bright green hulls. Always hull them after rinsing to keep them from becoming water-logged.*

# SUPPER ON A MOMENT'S NOTICE

TAGLIARINI WITH ARTICHOKE HEARTS
AND MUSHROOMS
SPIKED ORANGES
WHOLE WHEAT PECAN CAKE

◆

This is a contemporary pantry-shelf supper. The fresh pasta can be kept on hand in the freezer as can the artichoke hearts. (Frozen artichoke hearts have better texture than the canned ones.) Pecans, as well as other types of nuts, should also be stored in the freezer to prevent them from becoming stale or rancid. Some of the other fresh ingredients—garlic, parsley, and oranges—are items I always have on hand. Only the mushrooms require last-minute purchase, but in a pinch dried porcini or even Chinese black mushrooms, also pantry-shelf staples in my house, could be substituted.

Like so many of my menus, this one calls for preparing the dessert first, but it needn't be made much in advance because it requires minimal cooling before it is cut and served. The main dish requires only fifteen minutes from start to finish.

A light Italian white wine such as Galestro or pinot grigio would be the best choice with this menu. Artichokes tend to distort the flavor of wine but are less intrusive with one that is fairly neutral, with good acidity.

*Sautéed mushrooms and artichokes with tagliarini noodles make a quick supper.*

## TAGLIARINI WITH ARTICHOKE HEARTS AND MUSHROOMS

*Frozen artichoke hearts are marvelous for emergencies or last-minute dinners. Steam them just until they thaw, or defrost them in a microwave oven, then serve them with pasta or grains, in salads or soups.*

*Tagliarini is a cut of fresh pasta similar to fettuccine but thinner. In the local dialect of the Piedmont region of northwestern Italy, where this cut is extremely popular, often served just with butter and sage, it is called* tajarin. *If you do not have a supply of fresh tagliarini or fettuccine in your freezer, use regular packaged linguine instead.*

*Serves 3 to 4*

1 **package frozen artichoke hearts, defrosted**
6 **tablespoons extra-virgin olive oil**
2 **garlic cloves, minced**
4 **ounces fresh mushrooms, sliced**
   **Salt and freshly ground black pepper**
2 **tablespoons finely minced fresh Italian parsley**
9 **to 10 ounces fresh tagliarini (thin fettuccine)**
   **Freshly grated Parmesan cheese**

Spread the artichoke hearts on a paper towel to dry thoroughly.

Place a large, heavy skillet over medium heat. Add 3 tablespoons of the oil, then add the garlic and sauté a few seconds until golden. Increase heat to high, add the artichoke hearts, and sauté a few minutes, until lightly browned. Remove the artichokes from the pan, draining them well with a slotted spoon.

Add another tablespoon of oil to the pan. Add the mushrooms and sauté over high heat until lightly browned. Remove the pan from the heat and add the artichokes. Season to taste with salt and pepper. Stir in the parsley and the remaining oil.

Bring a large pot of salted water to a boil. Add the tagliarini and stir once or twice. Cook 2 to 3 minutes after the water returns to a boil, then drain the tagliarini.

Briefly reheat the mushrooms and artichokes. Toss with the tagliarini in a warm serving bowl. Serve with the cheese passed separately.

## SPIKED ORANGES

*Serves 4*

8 navel oranges
1 tablespoon honey
2 tablespoons dark rum
½ vanilla bean

Using a sharp knife, peel the oranges down to the flesh, holding them over a bowl to catch the juices. Be sure to remove all the white pith. Slice the oranges horizontally and remove any pits. Arrange the slices in a shallow bowl.

Drizzle the oranges with the honey and the rum. Split the vanilla bean and scrape the seeds over the oranges. Cover and refrigerate until ready to serve.

*This recipe calls for navel oranges, which are virtually seedless. Do use a real vanilla bean, rather than extract, so the seeds can speckle the dessert.*

## WHOLE WHEAT PECAN CAKE

*Serves 6*

1 cup very finely chopped pecans
1 cup whole wheat flour
1 teaspoon baking powder
4 tablespoons (½ stick) unsalted butter, softened
1 cup sugar
2 large eggs

Preheat the oven to 350°F. Grease and flour an 8-inch round baking pan.

In a small bowl, mix the pecans, flour, and baking powder. Set aside. In a larger bowl, cream the butter. Add the sugar, beating until the mixture is light and fluffy. Beat in the eggs one at a time. Fold in the pecan mixture.

Spread the batter in the pan and bake for 40 minutes, or until a cake tester comes out clean. Serve warm or cool.

*This is a plain, homey, but irresistible cake that is wonderful toasted with morning coffee in place of a muffin.*

*Pecans are among the oiliest of nuts, so chopping them fine without having them turn to a paste can be tricky. Storing them in the freezer and chopping them together with a few tablespoons of the sugar from the recipe helps.*

# A MIDSUMMER LUNCH

CHICK-PEA–OLIVADA SALAD
PAPPA AL POMODORO
WATERCRESS IN LEMON DRESSING
PRUNES IN CHIANTI

◆

**M**y friends and family would gladly eat this menu nearly every day. It is light yet satisfying, with a Tuscan "soup" of bread and tomatoes followed by a pair of savory salads, one with chick-peas and the other with watercress. Prunes, underappreciated as a dessert fruit in this country, are delicious soaked in wine.

Except for the watercress salad, the menu can be prepared early in the day. For last-minute timing, begin the preparation with the prunes.

The wine of choice for this menu is, of course, a robust Chianti.

*Pappa al pomodoro, the rustic Tuscan "bread soup"*
*with accompanying salads*

The purist will prepare this recipe with dried chick-peas; the pragmatist keeps canned cooked chick-peas in the pantry. Turn canned beans upside down before opening so none stick to the bottom and rinse the beans well. Black olive paste, called olivada, imported from Italy, is worth keeping on hand to season dips, salad dressings, and pasta sauces, and to spread on toast as a quick hors d'oeuvre.

Our newfound passion for Tuscan food has put pappa al pomodoro, literally tomato pap, on many American tables. It is a "bread soup," a type of dish popular not only in Italy but also in Spain and Portugal. In this dish the bread absorbs the liquid, making a thick, filling, porridgelike mass of rich tomatoes fragrant with garlic and basil. Adding bread to a soup mixture is a method of stretching leftovers in the peasant kitchen, but lately this dish has

## CHICK-PEA—OLIVADA SALAD

*Serves 4*

2 cups cooked chick-peas
1 garlic clove, finely minced
12 European-style black olives, pitted and halved
2 tablespoons minced scallion
1 tablespoon chopped Italian parsley
Juice of 1½ lemons
2 teaspoons olivada (black olive paste)
3 tablespoons extra-virgin olive oil
Freshly ground black pepper

Place the chick-peas in a bowl and gently mix in the garlic, olives, scallion, and parsley.

In a separate bowl, mix the lemon juice with the olivada and olive oil. Pour over the chick-peas and mix gently. Season to taste with pepper, mix again, and serve.

## PAPPA AL POMODORO

*Serves 4*

2 pounds ripe fresh tomatoes, seeds and cores removed
6 tablespoons extra-virgin olive oil
½ cup finely chopped onion
4 garlic cloves, chopped
1 piece day-old Italian bread (6 inches long), coarsely chopped
3 tablespoons finely chopped fresh basil
Salt and freshly ground black pepper
Basil leaves, for garnish

Coarsely chop the tomatoes, place in a food processor, and process until finely chopped but not pureed.

Heat half the oil in a large saucepan or skillet over medium heat. Add the onion and cook until soft but not brown. Stir in the garlic, sauté briefly, then add the tomatoes. Cook about 10 minutes, until the tomatoes are soft and thick. Remove from heat.

Crumble the bread into the tomato mixture. Mix, then add the basil and season to taste with salt and pepper. The mixture should be thick.

Serve at room temperature, garnished with basil leaves and with remaining olive oil drizzled over the top.

*become stylish and classy in its sublime simplicity. In a pinch, well-drained canned whole plum tomatoes can be substituted.*

## WATERCRESS IN LEMON DRESSING

*Serves 4*

1 **large bunch watercress, heavy stems discarded**
**Juice and grated rind of 1 lemon**
1 **teaspoon Dijon mustard**
2 **tablespoons extra-virgin olive oil**
**Freshly ground black pepper**

Place the watercress in a salad bowl. Mix the lemon juice, rind, and mustard in a bowl. Beat in the oil and season with pepper to taste. Pour the dressing over the watercress, toss, and serve.

*Other bitter or spicy greens such as dandelion, arugula, or mizuna can be substituted for the watercress. Choose watercress with crisp, dark green leaves and no sign of yellowing. Always remove any thick stems.*

## PRUNES IN CHIANTI

*Serves 4*

2 **cups pitted prunes**
¼ **teaspoon mace**
1 **cinnamon stick**
½ **lemon**
1 **cup Chianti or other dry red wine**
**Heavy cream or vanilla ice cream**

Place the prunes in a saucepan. Stir in the mace, cinnamon stick, lemon half, and wine. Bring to a simmer and cook very slowly for about 20 minutes, until the prunes are soft. Allow to cool to room temperature. Discard lemon half and cinnamon stick. Serve prunes with heavy cream or ice cream, if desired.

*Prunes in wine are served all over Europe, and with good reason—they are delicious. Americans indoctrinated only about the healthful attributes of prunes tend to neglect them.*

*Some specialty shops sell imported French Agen prunes. These are especially flavorful.*

# PASTA, PESTO, AND PEARS

ARUGULA SALAD WITH
PESTO VINAIGRETTE

PENNE WITH EGGPLANT,
TOMATOES, AND MOZZARELLA

LEMON-PEPPER PEARS SPLASHED
WITH GRAPPA

◆

This menu is another favorite for quick suppers or weekend lunches. Invariably, I can find an eggplant and some fresh mozzarella in a nearby store. Finding decent plum tomatoes seems to be easier, on a year-round basis, than having ripe regular tomatoes on hand, but well-drained canned tomatoes are an acceptable substitute.

Begin preparation with the dessert, then make the vinaigrette and rinse the salad ingredients. Then you can devote your attention to the pasta and its vegetable-based sauce.

I consider this a red wine meal, calling for a Chianti or an undemanding cabernet sauvignon from California. Beer would also be appropriate.

*Pears poached with lemon and pepper and splashed with grappa*

## ARUGULA SALAD WITH PESTO VINAIGRETTE

*I usually have a batch of pesto in my refrigerator or freezer, ready to use. But for those times when I do not, and I need only a little, I have devised this method of making a small amount of pesto when that is all a recipe requires.*

### Serves 4

2 bunches arugula
1 garlic clove
1 tablespoon pine nuts
¼ cup fresh basil leaves, packed
¼ cup extra-virgin olive oil
2 tablespoons white wine vinegar

Rinse the arugula and remove all heavy stems. Dry the leaves well and place in a salad bowl.

With the food processor running, drop the garlic clove and pine nuts through the feed tube and process until they are finely chopped. Stuff the basil leaves through the feed tube and continue to process until they are chopped. Stop the machine and scrape the sides of the container.

With the machine running, add the olive oil slowly through the feed tube, then the vinegar. Pour the dressing over the arugula and serve.

## PENNE WITH EGGPLANT, TOMATOES, AND MOZZARELLA

*There is a world of difference between the freshly made mozzarella, with its moist creaminess, and the rubbery plastic-wrapped variety. Fortunately, these days even supermarkets often carry better, fresh mozzarella. As for buffalo mozzarella, so named because it is made from water buffalo milk in southern Italy (and not because it comes from upstate New*

### Serves 4

1 large eggplant, about 1 pound
1½ pounds plum tomatoes
3 tablespoons extra-virgin olive oil
1 small onion, diced
4 garlic cloves, minced
Salt and freshly ground black pepper
1 pound penne
8 ounces fresh mozzarella, shredded
¼ cup finely shredded basil leaves

Slice the stem end off the eggplant and cut the eggplant into 1-inch dice. Finely dice the tomatoes.

Heat the oil in a large, heavy skillet. Add the onion and sauté over medium heat for about 5 minutes, until soft but not brown. Stir in the garlic. Add the eggplant, increase the heat to medium-high, and sauté, stirring, until the eggplant looks moist, 5 to 7 minutes. Add the tomatoes.

Lower the heat and cook until the tomatoes soften, about 10 minutes. Season to taste with salt and pepper. Remove from heat.

Meanwhile, bring a large pot of salted water to a boil. Cook the penne about 8 minutes, until al dente.

Drain the penne, add to the eggplant mixture, and toss over low heat. Add the basil and mozzarella, toss again, and serve at once.

*York, like the chicken wings), it is delicious, but beware! It may not be fresh enough. It depends on your purveyor. You are better off buying good, fresh cow's-milk mozzarella.*

## LEMON-PEPPER PEARS SPLASHED WITH GRAPPA

*Serves 4*

4 pears, slightly underripe
Juice of 3 lemons
2 cups dry white wine
1 cup sugar
2 cups water
½ teaspoon whole peppercorns
3 tablespoons grappa or pear *eau-de-vie*

Peel the pears, cut them in half vertically, and remove the cores. Place them in a bowl with the juice of ½ lemon and enough water to cover. Set aside.

Place the remaining lemon juice in a large, heavy, nonaluminum saucepan along with the wine, sugar, water, and peppercorns. Bring to a boil, lower the heat, and simmer 20 minutes. Drain the pears and add them. Simmer 10 to 15 minutes longer, until the pears are just tender. Transfer the pears to a bowl with a slotted spoon.

Boil down the cooking liquid until it is reduced to about ¾ cup, about 10 minutes. Remove from the heat and stir in the grappa. Pour this syrup over the pears and allow to cool to room temperature before serving.

*A deliciously ripe pear is one of the joys of late summer or autumn. For those pears that are not quite ready for eating out of hand, here is a delightfully different dessert recipe.*

*The alcohol in the syrup is grappa, an eau-de-vie distilled in Italy from the lees of wine grapes. If grappa is unavailable, the pear eau-de-vie Poire Williams makes an admirable substitute. This dish can be refrigerated up to 24 hours.*

# A WINTER SUPPER

RYE AND FENNEL BREAD
SMOKED TROUT CHOWDER
RED CABBAGE SLAW
ROASTED APPLES WITH BROWN SUGAR GLAZE

◆

Essentially a soup-and-bread supper that might be spread on a farmhouse table in the northern Midwest, this is a menu to ward off winter's chill. The soup, a chunky chowder, is made with smoked fish instead of fresh clams or blackfish as it might be in New England. The earthy dark bread is of Scandinavian origin. It should be made in advance, but if time is of the essence, a substantial dark bread from a good bakery can replace it.

The crunch of red cabbage in the slaw is mellowed with raspberry vinegar and only a touch of sugar. The apples roasted in thick slices are easier to cook, to serve, and to eat than traditional baked apples served whole. Prepare the slaw, then the apples before starting the chowder.

Although a fruity white wine—a riesling or gewürztraminer from Washington State or a riesling kabinett from the Mosel area of Germany, for example— would complement this menu, it would also be excellent with beer or hard cider.

*Roasted apple slices glazed with brown sugar in an earthenware*
*casserole warm from the oven*

*M*any years ago I inter-
viewed a Finnish cook. Of
the recipes we discussed, this one
for a dark, moist, subtly spiced loaf
was the most appealing, and it has
endured in my repertory. Ground
fennel is sold in well-stocked spice
departments, but you can make it
yourself simply by grinding whole
fennel seeds in a spice mill. Medium or dark rye flour, not light,
is preferable for this bread.

## RYE AND FENNEL BREAD

*Makes 2 loaves*

1 package active dry yeast
⅓ cup warm milk (105°–115°F.)
½ cup molasses
1 tablespoon grated orange peel
1 tablespoon salt
1½ teaspoons ground fennel seeds
2 cups dark beer
½ cup old-fashioned rolled oats
½ cup oat bran
2½ cups medium or dark rye flour
1½ cups whole wheat flour
1 cup all-purpose flour (approximately)
2 teaspoons whole fennel seeds

Dissolve the yeast in the milk. Set aside in a warm place to proof, about 5 minutes.

Combine all but 1 tablespoon of the molasses with the orange peel, salt, and ground fennel seeds in a saucepan. Bring to a boil, then transfer to a large bowl and mix with the beer. Mix the remaining tablespoon of molasses with a tablespoon of warm water and set aside to use as a glaze.

Add the yeast mixture to the large bowl, then stir in the oats, bran, and rye flour. Add the whole wheat flour, ½ cup at a time, to make a soft, somewhat sticky dough.

Turn the dough out onto a board liberally covered with the all-purpose flour. Knead until the dough is soft, smooth, and fairly elastic, adding more all-purpose flour as necessary. Most of the stickiness should be gone from the dough.

Place the dough in an oiled bowl, cover, and set aside to rise until doubled, 1½ to 2 hours. Punch dough down, knead briefly, and divide in half. Shape each portion of dough into a narrow, plump oval and press half the fennel seeds into the top of each loaf. Place loaves on an oiled baking sheet and set aside to rise until doubled, about 1 hour.

Preheat the oven to 375°F. Brush each loaf with some of the molasses glaze. Place the sheet in the middle of the oven and bake until the loaves sound hollow when tapped, about 45 minutes. Brush more glaze on the loaves once or twice during baking.

Cover the loaves loosely with foil and cool on racks before slicing.

## SMOKED TROUT CHOWDER

*Serves 8*

3 tablespoons unsalted butter
1 cup chopped leeks, mostly the white part
2½ cups diced, peeled boiling potatoes
6 cups milk
4 smoked trout, about 7 ounces each, skinned and boned
Salt and freshly ground pepper
½ cup heavy cream
½ cup whipped cream
1 tablespoon prepared horseradish

*E*ssentially a recipe for New England clam chowder, this hearty soup can be varied at will. Smoked fish gives it a richly haunting flavor, but fresh fish such as blackfish, hake, or Pacific black cod can be substituted. Puree the smoked fish chowder in a blender, add more cream, and you have an elegant dinner-party soup.

Heat the butter in a large, heavy saucepan. Sauté the leeks until tender but not brown, about 8 minutes.

Add the potatoes and half the milk and simmer until the potatoes are tender, about 30 minutes.

Roughly mash the potatoes with a fork, leaving some pieces, then add the remaining milk. Break the fish into 1-inch pieces and add them to the saucepan. (As the soup cooks and is stirred, the pieces will break up.)

Simmer for 15 minutes. Taste for seasoning, adding salt if necessary and pepper generously. Stir in the cream.

Mix the whipped cream and horseradish in a bowl and top each serving with a dollop of the horseradish cream.

*Unlike a traditional creamy coleslaw, this one is dressed with a vinaigrette, subtly sweetened with a touch of sugar and raspberry vinegar. Like most slaws, it improves as the cabbage absorbs the dressing, so do not hesitate to prepare it in advance.*

## RED CABBAGE SLAW

*Serves 8*

1 small head red cabbage, about 1 pound
1 medium onion, sliced paper thin
Salt
½ teaspoon sugar
½ cup coarsely chopped Italian parsley leaves, packed
¼ cup raspberry vinegar
¼ cup extra-virgin olive oil
Freshly ground black pepper

Quarter the cabbage vertically and slice off the thick core. Using a knife or the fine slicing blade of a food processor, slice the cabbage very fine. In a large bowl, mix cabbage with the onion, sprinkle with about ½ teaspoon salt and the sugar, and, if time permits, allow to sit at room temperature for 1 hour.

Drain excess fluid, then fold in the parsley. Mix the vinegar and oil, and pour over the slaw. Toss. Season to taste with pepper and, if necessary, additional salt.

## ROASTED APPLES WITH BROWN SUGAR GLAZE

*Serves 8*

8 medium Granny Smith apples
3 tablespoons unsalted butter
1¼ cups packed light brown sugar
1 teaspoon ground cinnamon
Juice of 2 lemons
Whipped cream, crème fraîche, or vanilla ice cream

Peel the apples. Cut each in half horizontally and, using an apple corer or a paring knife, remove the cores.

Place 2 tablespoons of the butter in a shallow baking dish, preferably glass, that is large enough to hold

the apples in a single layer. You will need a dish at least 9 × 13 inches. Place the dish in the oven and preheat the oven to 350°F. When the butter has melted, remove the dish from the oven and mix 1 cup of the brown sugar and the cinnamon with the melted butter in the dish.

Arrange the apples in the dish, sprinkle them with the remaining sugar and the lemon juice, and dot with the remaining butter. Bake for 1 hour, 15 minutes, turning apple pieces and basting them with the pan juices once or twice during baking. By the time they are tender they should be well glazed, and the juices in the pan should be thick and syrupy.

Baste the apples once more and allow to cool for 20 to 30 minutes. Serve directly from the dish or transfer them to a serving platter, basting again with the syrup. Serve whipped cream, crème fraîche, or ice cream on the side.

*The typically large baked apple leaves something to be desired in my view—something aesthetic, that is. Thick slices of baked apple make for a more attractive presentation with more of the deliciously syrupy brown sugar glaze per bite. Use a fairly dry-textured tart apple; Granny Smith is best, but Cortland or Mutsu are good substitutes.*

# ASIAN STREET FOOD

SCALLOP AND BROCCOLI SALAD
DUCK LO MEIN
SUGAR SNAP STIR-FRY
MANGOES WITH MANGO SORBET

◆

This is another menu that calls for an Asian larder: soy sauce, oyster sauce, hot sauce, fish sauce, rice vinegar, and oriental sesame oil are some of its components. But these ingredients are well worth keeping on hand to use in seasonings and dressings.

Preparation of the menu should begin with the tangy, tart-sweet sorbet. The main course comes next, but once the duck breast has been par-cooked, the lo mein is essentially a last-minute dish. It is the sort of hearty, earthy noodle preparation typically sold in street stalls throughout Asia and, as such, is also appropriate for advance preparation and reheating. The first course salad and the crunchy, verdant Sugar Snap peas are ready in minutes.

Beer; a white wine like gewürztraminer that has some spice; or a fruity red such as a young zinfandel from California, a shiraz from Australia, or a Côtes-du-Rhône from France would best complement the menu.

## SCALLOP AND BROCCOLI SALAD

*Serves 4*

2 cups very small broccoli flowerets
½ pound sea scallops
6 tablespoons oriental sesame oil
1 teaspoon minced fresh ginger
⅓ cup finely chopped scallions
1½ teaspoons light soy sauce
1 tablespoon oyster sauce
2 tablespoons rice vinegar
   Few drops Chinese hot pepper oil, to taste
1 tablespoon sesame seeds
1 bunch watercress, rinsed, dried, and trimmed
   of heavy stems

Steam the broccoli for 1 minute, refresh under cold water, then drain. Place in a large bowl.

Dry the scallops. Brush them with 3 tablespoons of the sesame oil, then broil or grill them for about 3 minutes at very high heat. The scallops can also be seared in a very hot cast-iron skillet that has been wiped with vegetable oil. Place the scallops in the bowl with the broccoli, add the ginger and scallions, and mix gently.

In a small bowl, combine the soy sauce, oyster sauce, rice vinegar, remaining sesame oil, and hot pepper oil to taste. Mix well, then stir in the sesame seeds.

Not more than 1 hour before serving, mix the scallops and broccoli with the dressing. Divide the watercress among 4 plates and arrange the salad on the watercress. Serve at once.

*Like most green vegetables, broccoli contains an enzyme that reacts with acid and dulls its color. For this reason it is important not to add the dressing more than one hour before the salad will be served.*

*The salad specifies large sea scallops, which will take on a little color under the broiler or on a grill without becoming overcooked.*

The finished dish looks like what Chinese restaurants call lo mein (and also tastes something like it), but this dish is actually from Burma, now known as Myanmar. It was adapted from a recipe for "street market noodles" with duck given to me by Irene Khin Wong, a charming woman who owned a restaurant in Manhattan. The fish sauce and garnish of fried onions are classic Burmese touches.

The duck breast used is simply the breast section of a regular Pekin or Long Island duckling. Freeze the back and legs for making Duck Rillettes (page 227).

**Duck lo mein, "street food," with Sugar Snap peas**

## DUCK LO MEIN

*Serves 4 to 6*

1 breast of duck (with bone)
½ pound fresh Chinese egg noodles or other fresh thin egg pasta
¼ cup peanut oil
½ cup thinly sliced onion
2 tablespoons minced fresh ginger
3 garlic cloves, minced
½ cup chopped scallions
1 teaspoon dark soy sauce
1 teaspoon light soy sauce
1 tablespoon Thai fish sauce (*nuoc mam*)
Freshly ground black pepper

Place the duck breast in a pan with water to cover and simmer over medium heat for 7 minutes. Drain and set aside until cool enough to handle.

Bring 4 cups of water to a boil in a large pot. Add the noodles and cook for 3 minutes, stirring constantly. Drain, rinse thoroughly under cold water, drain again, and place in a colander lined with paper towels to dry.

When the duck is cool enough to handle, remove the skin and bones and slice the meat in thin strips. Set aside.

Heat 1 tablespoon of the peanut oil in a wok or skillet. Sauté the onion until golden, then remove from the pan and place on paper towels to drain. Add the remaining oil to the wok or skillet, stir-fry the ginger and garlic for a few seconds, then add the duck and stir-fry until it loses its redness, a few minutes. Add all but 1 tablespoon of the scallions.

Add the noodles to the pan and mix well. Add the soy sauces and the fish sauce, and season liberally with pepper. Toss to combine the ingredients.

Transfer the noodles to a serving platter, sprinkle with the remaining scallions and the fried onions, and serve.

*W*hat did we ever do before Sugar Snap peas? Introduced shortly after Chinese snow peas became widely available, this hybrid is a cross between snow peas and regular garden peas, with fully edible pods that are sweeter than snow peas and have more crunch. They are good raw or cooked.

## SUGAR SNAP STIR-FRY

*Serves 4 to 6*

¾ pound Sugar Snap peas
½ tablespoon peanut oil
1 teaspoon minced fresh ginger
½ tablespoon oriental sesame oil
Pinch of sugar
Pinch of salt

Pull any stems off the Sugar Snap peas. Heat the peanut oil in a wok or a heavy skillet. Add the ginger, stir-fry for a few seconds, then add the peas and stir-fry until they turn very bright green. Season with sesame oil, sugar, and salt. Serve hot or at room temperature.

*W*hole mangoes are beautiful, their green skin blushed with rose. The juicy orange flesh is tart-sweet.

The best way to slice a mango is to cut it horizontally, not quite in half, separating all the flesh on one side of the pit. Repeat for the other half. Peel and dice as much of the flesh as possible clinging to the pit, then scoop or slice the flesh away from the leathery skin of the two halves.

## MANGOES WITH MANGO SORBET

*Serves 6*

3 large mangoes
⅓ cup sugar
3 tablespoons fresh lime juice

Peel and dice the flesh from 1½ of the mangoes and puree in a food processor. You should have about 1½ cups of puree. Dissolve the sugar in the lime juice, mix with the mango puree, and return the mixture to the food processor to process briefly. Freeze in an ice cream freezer according to the manufacturer's directions.

Peel and slice the remaining mangoes and arrange on plates. Top with the sorbet.

# LAST-MINUTE SUPPER

QUICK CHICKEN BREASTS WITH
PEPPER AND TOMATO TOPPING
ORZO WITH PARMESAN CHEESE AND SAGE
RASPBERRY PARFAITS

◆

The lineup of dishes for this menu sounds more elaborate than it is, considering a well-organized cook can handle it in about thirty minutes. And, except for the raspberries, it is based on ingredients that are reliably in the market all year round. Although designed as supper for two, it could be doubled with ease and even suits a dinner party.

In many ways I consider this an ideal menu, not only because shopping for the ingredients makes no undue demands on a busy cook at any time of year and because it can be prepared in under an hour, but also because of the balance in its design.

Rather than a sauce, chicken breasts are given a savory relishlike topping. Orzo, a rice-shaped pasta, comes dusted with sage and fresh Parmesan cheese in typically northern Italian fashion, providing starch plus a savory and herbaceous counterpoint.

The raspberries, an indulgence for two, is an extravagant gesture when guests are involved. If need be, of course, other fruits could be served in the parfaits.

With this menu I pour a medium-bodied, smooth red wine, such as Inferno from Lombardy, a red Rioja from Spain, or a merlot from California.

*Chicken breasts with pepper
and tomato topping and orzo with
Parmesan cheese and sage for supper*

## QUICK CHICKEN BREASTS WITH PEPPER AND TOMATO TOPPING

*While chicken breasts may not have a great deal of personality, they certainly are convenient, versatile, and easy to cook. This recipe calls for them to be topped with a savory sweet pepper-and-tomato mixture.*

*Serves 2*

1 tablespoon extra-virgin olive oil
Juice of 1 lemon
½ teaspoon dried sage
Freshly ground black pepper
4 skinless, boneless chicken breasts (¾ pound)
1 small red bell pepper, seeded and finely chopped
6 ounces ripe plum tomatoes, finely chopped
2 scallions, minced
Hot red pepper flakes

Combine 1 teaspoon of the olive oil with the lemon juice, sage, and pepper to taste in a shallow dish. Add the chicken breasts, turn them once to coat them, and set them aside to marinate for 15 minutes.

While the chicken is marinating, heat the remaining oil in a nonstick skillet. Add the red pepper and tomatoes, and cook over medium-high heat for 5 to 10 minutes, until they have reduced to a thick sauce. Add the scallions, cook a moment longer, then season with hot pepper flakes. Remove the tomato mixture from the skillet.

In the same skillet, sauté the chicken breasts for about 5 minutes on each side, until just cooked through. Transfer the chicken to a serving plate or individual plates. Return the tomato mixture to the skillet to reheat briefly, then spoon over the chicken and serve.

## ORZO WITH PARMESAN CHEESE AND SAGE

*Serves 2*

½ **cup orzo**
  **Salt and freshly ground black pepper**
2 **tablespoons unsalted butter or extra-virgin olive oil**
1 **tablespoon minced fresh sage**
2 **tablespoons freshly grated Parmesan cheese**

Bring 1 quart of salted water to a boil and add the orzo. Boil until just tender, about 8 minutes. Drain. Season to taste with salt and pepper.

Just before serving, melt the butter in a skillet. Add the orzo and sage, and toss to combine the ingredients and reheat the orzo. Transfer the orzo to a serving dish or individual plates, sprinkle with the cheese, and serve.

*Unlike many pastas, orzo is best served as a side dish; it is not substantial enough to serve topped with a sauce as a separate course. Orzo cooks in a trice and can be dressed with various seasonings. Here it is served with butter, fresh sage, and a dusting of Parmesan cheese, one of the more felicitous combinations popular in northern Italy.*

## RASPBERRY PARFAITS

*Serves 2*

½ **pint fresh raspberries**
4 **teaspoons light brown sugar**
4 **ounces whole-milk, goat's-milk, or sheep's-milk yogurt**

Place half the raspberries in each of 2 large wine goblets. Sprinkle each portion with 1 teaspoon of the sugar.

Gently stir the yogurt to smooth it, then spoon it over the berries. Add the remaining berries and brown sugar and serve.

*One precious half-pint of raspberries is an indulgence for two. Savor the berries plain or layered with yogurt and brown sugar. If calories are not a consideration, substitute crème fraîche for the yogurt for an even more decadent treat.*

# A LIGHT SUMMER MENU

GRILLED BUTTERMILK QUAIL
WITH ONIONS
WILD RICE AND CORN SALAD
BIBB LETTUCE SALAD
BLUEBERRIES IN GIN

◆

The simplicity of this lunch or supper is in its preparation; it sounds more elaborate than it is. The butterflied quail are marinated for a couple of hours or even overnight, then grilled in a twinkling. And once the quail have begun marinating, the entire meal can be assembled in less than an hour. The wild rice salad can be prepared in advance or not, as convenience dictates. Ditto, the blueberries and the salad dressing.

My choice of wine is a light red such as a pinot noir from California or Oregon, a simple Côtes de Beaune-Villages, or one of the many well-made Bordeaux from the less-exalted estates.

*Wild rice and corn salad to accompany grilled quail*

## GRILLED BUTTERMILK QUAIL
## WITH ONIONS

*Serves 6 to 8*

16 quail
2 cups buttermilk
1½ teaspoons hot pepper sauce
3 to 4 large sweet onions, such as Vidalia, sliced
¼ cup balsamic vinegar

Butterfly the quail by snipping up the backbone with shears, then flattening them. Place in a large dish.

Mix the buttermilk with 1¼ teaspoons hot pepper sauce and pour over the quail, coating them well. Cover and refrigerate overnight, up to 24 hours.

Preheat the grill or broiler. Grill or broil the quail close to the source of heat until lightly browned, 3 to 5 minutes on each side. While the quail are grilling, dip the onion slices in the buttermilk marinade. Grill the onion slices a minute or two on each side.

Arrange the onions on a platter and top with the quail. Mix the vinegar with the remaining ¼ teaspoon hot pepper sauce, sprinkle over the quail, and serve.

## WILD RICE AND CORN SALAD

*Serves 6 to 8*

1 cup wild rice
3 cups water
1½ cups cooked corn kernels, preferably fresh
¾ cup finely chopped tomato
1 teaspoon finely chopped fresh hot chili pepper
2 scallions, chopped
1 tablespoon Dijon mustard
1 tablespoon honey
⅓ cup cider vinegar
¼ cup extra-virgin olive oil
Salt

*It's a fallacy that game is best enjoyed in fall, the hunting season. Game can be hunted in season for personal use, but it is illegal to sell it in stores or restaurants, and virtually all of the game on today's table has been raised on farms. It is available year-round, is tender, and does not have that characteristic gamy flavor.*

*This recipe is typically Southern. The Vidalia onions, sweet onions from Georgia, are a Southern specialty. Others, like Maui, Walla Walla, or Texas Super Sweet onions can be substituted.*

*Wild rice's chewy texture allows it to sop up a dressing without becoming soggy, making it excellent for salads. As with white rice, allowing it to rest, covered, for several minutes after cooking improves the rice's texture and makes it fluffier.*

Place the rice in a saucepan with the water and bring to a boil. Lower the heat and simmer for 45 minutes. Cover the pan, remove from heat, and set aside for 10 minutes longer. Transfer the rice to a bowl, then add the corn, tomato, chili pepper, and scallions and mix well.

Beat the mustard and honey together in a small bowl. Beat in the vinegar and olive oil. Pour over the rice mixture and mix gently. Season with salt. Allow to marinate at room temperature at least 1 hour before serving.

## BIBB LETTUCE SALAD

*Serves 6 to 8*

¼ **cup white wine vinegar**
2 **teaspoons Dijon mustard**
1 **garlic clove, minced**
½ **cup extra-virgin olive oil**
   **Salt and freshly ground black pepper**
1 **tablespoon finely minced fresh mint leaves**
1 **tablespoon minced fresh chives**
3 **to 4 heads Bibb lettuce, rinsed and dried**

*Small heads of Bibb lettuce, sometimes called Kentucky Limestone, may have been the first of the baby lettuces. Tiny leaves of other, newer kinds of baby lettuce such as Lolla Rossa or the mixtures of tender greens called mesclun can be used with or instead of the Bibb. Mint adds a delightfully refreshing flavor.*

Beat the vinegar and mustard together. Add the garlic, then beat in the oil. Season with salt and pepper.

Arrange the greens in a salad bowl, pour the dressing over the lettuce, and toss. Add the herbs and toss thoroughly.

## BLUEBERRIES IN GIN

*Serves 6 to 8*

2 **pints fresh blueberries**
½ **cup gin**
2 **to 4 tablespoons sugar**

*Gin, with its vegetal, juniper flavor, is an excellent complement for blueberries.*

Rinse and pick over the blueberries. Toss with the gin and sugar to taste. Serve in goblets.

# HOLIDAY AND BUFFET ENTERTAINING

Special-occasion family dinners and buffets for a crowd call for cooking in quantity, often complicating the marketing and the preparation. On the other hand, serving such menus can be done more informally than a regular dinner party, making the party easier on the host or hostess once guests have arrived.

Holiday dinners usually are family occasions. The guest list consists of relatives and perhaps a few friends who have been close to the family. A regular dinner party might involve the same number of guests, but when it's family the list takes less meticulous planning. Invariably we know in advance who to include.

As for the menus, they combine an unmistakably traditional approach with some imaginative touches. The foods tend to be more substantial than fancy. A buffet spread is my favorite scheme for entertaining twelve or more guests. With that many, buffet is easier for everyone. I spend less time doing the actual serving, guests can help themselves to exactly what they wish to eat, and everyone is free to refill his or her plate at will.

There is a difference between buffet food and plated dinner food. For convenience I might serve the main course of a sit-down dinner party *buffet style, allowing guests to take their plates from the table, help themselves, and then return to their places at the table, but that's not what I mean by a buffet. At a buffet party the dining table often becomes the serving table. A stack of plates waits at one end, along with a pile of knives and forks wrapped in napkins. Sometimes I put these in a pretty basket.*

*For buffet service the food must be chosen with care. It should look colorful and abundant. Ease of self-service is important unless you have ample staff. If guests are all to be seated at tables, the choice of dishes is more flexible than if they will be perched around the house, balancing plates on their laps or on any available surface. In the latter situation, be sure to provide generous cloth napkins and either bite-size or finger food that can be managed without a knife, or a dish such as fish that can be cut with a fork. The spicy Jamaican-style chicken or the grand aïoli are also good options.*

*Finally, the best food for a buffet is a selection of dishes that are palatable and remain attractive when left at room temperature. The buffet menus in this chapter comply with these requirements.*

# A FESTIVE LUNCHEON

CHEESE TOASTS

WARM GRILLED SHRIMP, SCALLOP,
AND ENDIVE SALAD

WHEAT BERRY SALAD

STRAWBERRY-RHUBARB COBBLER

◆

Warm open-face melted cheese hors d'oeuvre are the inviting beginning for this lunch, which would be delightful served on a sunny terrace or balcony. The main course is a salad of grilled seafood and endive served warm along with a colorful wheat berry salad that offers a bit of earthy crunch. Dessert is an American classic.

The wheat berry salad and dessert are best if prepared in advance. The cheese toasts and the seafood and endive salad require last-minute attention.

A white wine with a fruity richness such as a riesling would best complement the menu.

*Warm grilled shrimp, scallop, and endive salad*

## CHEESE TOASTS

### Serves 6

**6 slices Egg Bread (page 210), each ½ inch thick**
**3 tablespoons unsalted butter, softened**
**⅓ cup freshly grated imported Italian Parmesan cheese**

*These cheese toasts are offered with cocktails at Le Cirque, one of the country's outstanding restaurants. The rich egg bread nicely complements the dryness of the cheese. Brioche or challah are good substitutes for homemade egg bread.*

Cut each slice of bread in half on the diagonal and toast lightly on both sides. Spread with the butter.

Sprinkle each piece with some of the Parmesan cheese. Place under the broiler for about 30 seconds, just until the cheese melts. Arrange on a serving plate and serve.

## WARM GRILLED SHRIMP, SCALLOP, AND ENDIVE SALAD

### Serves 6

**Juice of 2 lemons**
**½ cup extra-virgin olive oil**
**3 garlic cloves, minced**
**½ teaspoon fennel seeds, lightly crushed**
**Salt and freshly ground black pepper**
**1¼ pounds large shrimp, shelled and deveined**
**1¼ pounds sea scallops, of uniform size**
**¾ pound Belgian endive**
**½ teaspoon Dijon mustard**
**½ cup coarsely chopped Italian parsley**

*Only large sea scallops will do for this recipe. These are the most succulent and, in my opinion, the tastiest of the various kinds of scallops. Genuine bay scallops, which average three-quarters of an inch in diameter and come mostly from Long Island, New England, and Washington, are also very good, but they should not be confused with tiny calicos, often mislabeled as bay scallops. Those are a type of sea scallop dredged offshore in Georgia and Florida and steamed out of their shells, and they tend to be tasteless.*

Mix the juice of 1 lemon with 3 tablespoons of the oil, 2 garlic cloves, the fennel seeds, and salt and pepper to taste in a large glass or ceramic bowl. Add the shrimp and scallops and toss to coat. Marinate in the refrigerator, covered, for 1 hour.

Preheat a grill or broiler.

Slice the heads of endive in half lengthwise. Do not remove the cores. Place about 1½ tablespoons of the olive oil in a shallow bowl and roll the endive in it to coat it thoroughly. Grill or broil the endive a few minutes on each side until the edges of the leaves begin to brown. Remove the endive, cut away the cores, chop leaves coarsely, and place in a salad bowl or serving dish.

Remove the shrimp and scallops from the marinade. Oil a rack to go on the grill that will hold them without falling through or thread them on skewers. Grill or broil a few minutes on each side until they are just cooked through and beginning to brown on the edges.

Add the shrimp and scallops to the dish with the endive, cutting any very large scallops in half.

Mix the remaining 3½ tablespoons of olive oil with the juice of 1 lemon, the remaining clove of garlic, and the mustard. Season to taste with salt and pepper and pour over the seafood and endive. Toss gently. Add the parsley, toss again, and serve while still warm.

## WHEAT BERRY SALAD

*Serves 6*

1½ **cups wheat berries**
  3 **red bell peppers, cored, seeded, and finely chopped**
  2 **tablespoons lemon juice**
  3 **tablespoons extra-virgin olive oil**
    **Salt and freshly ground black pepper**

Place the wheat berries in a saucepan with water to cover by a depth of 1 inch. Bring to a boil and simmer for 2 minutes, then set aside for 1 hour.

After soaking, add additional water to the wheat berries so they are again covered to a depth of 1 inch. Bring to a simmer, cover, and cook gently until the wheat berries are tender, about 45 minutes. Drain well and place in a serving dish. Cool to room temperature.

Fold in the red peppers, lemon juice, and olive oil. Season to taste with salt and pepper and serve.

*D*ried whole wheat berries are the first step, so to speak, once wheat has been harvested. When cracked, the berries become bulghur, and when ground, the result is whole wheat flour. Eliminate the germ and the bran, and you have white flour.

Cooking wheat berries is like preparing dried beans: soak and simmer. If time is of the essence, bulghur can be substituted.

## STRAWBERRY-RHUBARB COBBLER

*Serves 6 to 8*

1½ cups light brown sugar, packed
2 tablespoons cornstarch
3 cups scraped rhubarb, in 1-inch pieces
1 pint ripe strawberries, hulled and halved
4 tablespoons (½ stick) unsalted butter, melted
½ teaspoon ground cinnamon
1 cup self-rising flour
¼ teaspoon salt
5 tablespoons cold unsalted butter
3 to 4 tablespoons milk
1 tablespoon granulated sugar
Whipped cream

*I have to feel that the seasonal coincidence of strawberries and rhubarb, both springtime crops, is what accounts for the combination in so many recipes. The sweetness of the berries superbly complements the tartness of the rhubarb. Never use rhubarb leaves: they contain oxalic acid and are toxic.*

Preheat the oven to 350°F. Butter an 8-inch square or a 9-inch round baking dish that is attractive enough to go to the table.

Mix the brown sugar with the cornstarch in a large bowl. Fold in the rhubarb, strawberries, melted butter, and cinnamon. Spoon this mixture into the baking dish.

Mix the flour and salt. Cut in the cold butter until the mixture has the texture of coarse meal. (This step can be done in a food processor.) Lightly stir in the milk to form a firm but tender dough. Roll out the dough on a floured board and cut it into strips 1 inch wide. Criss-cross the strips over the fruit. Sprinkle the top with the granulated sugar.

Bake for about 40 minutes, or until the crust has browned and the filling bubbles. Serve while still warm, topped with whipped cream.

# A FAMILY-STYLE SUNDAY DINNER MENU

HOT-HOT TOMATO BROTH
KASHA WITH MUSHROOMS
LIGHTENED CREAMED SPINACH
OLD-FASHIONED POT ROAST
CRANBERRY PICKLE
FRUIT COMPOTE STEEPED IN TEA
DEEP CHOCOLATE CHUNK LOAF

◆

This hearty family menu offers a number of all-time crowd pleasers. My husband adores a succulent pot roast, but it's a dish I reserve for colder weather when there will be more than four at the table. The earthy and homey kasha, creamed spinach, and a chocolate cake make this a popular menu, and there are often requests for second helpings of the spicy soup and the hauntingly fragrant fruit compote, too!

It pays to prepare the pot roast a day in advance. Similarly, although the tangy sweet-tart cranberry pickle can be served almost immediately, it's better if allowed to cure at least overnight or even as long as several weeks. The chocolate cake, the compote, the soup, and the spinach can be made early in the day or the day before the dinner. The kasha can be prepared in advance and reheated, or cooked during the hour before dinner, while the meal is being assembled.

This is a red wine dinner, suitable for as fine a Bordeaux, a California cabernet sauvignon, or a Barolo from Italy as your family would appreciate.

*When I use canned plum tomatoes I frequently drain them well, mashing them gently as they sit in a sieve, to obtain a thick pulp. Instead of discarding the liquid I freeze it in quart-size plastic containers to use in soups or as the cooking liquid for rice or other grains. Look for San Marzano tomatoes that have not been processed with salt or citric acid.*

## HOT-HOT TOMATO BROTH

*Serves 8*

**8 cups liquid drained from canned plum tomatoes,
  or 8 cups fresh or canned tomato juice
1 teaspoon ground ginger
½ to 1 teaspoon hot pepper sauce
  Salt and freshly ground black pepper
½ cup sour cream**

If there are any seeds in the juice, strain them out. Place the juice in a large saucepan and bring to a simmer over medium heat.

In a small cup, mix the ginger with about 1 tablespoon of the hot broth, then stir the mixture back into the soup. Season the soup with hot pepper sauce, then salt and pepper to taste. Garnish with a dollop of sour cream.

*The conventional directions for cooking kasha call for coating the groats with beaten egg, then cooking them in a dry saucepan before adding the liquid. This method keeps them fluffy and separate. But I discovered, while working on an article about buckwheat for the New York Times, that it's not necessary to use a whole egg. In this era of cholesterol-concern, just the egg white*

## KASHA WITH MUSHROOMS

*Serves 8*

**2 tablespoons olive oil or unsalted butter
2 cups finely chopped onions
1½ pounds mushrooms, chopped finely
1 egg white
1½ cups coarse or medium-grain kasha
2⅔ cups beef or chicken stock
  Salt and freshly ground black pepper**

Heat the oil or butter in a heavy 3- to 4-quart saucepan. Add the onions and sauté over medium heat, stirring from time to time, about 10 to 15 minutes, until they just begin to color. Add the mushrooms and sauté the mixture, stirring, until the mushrooms release their liquid, the liquid evaporates, and the mushrooms begin to brown, about 10 minutes longer.

Beat the egg white in a bowl until it looks bubbly. Stir in the kasha and mix well to coat the grains. Add the kasha to the saucepan and stir over medium heat until the grains look separate, 2 to 3 minutes.

Bring the stock to a boil in a separate pan, stir it into the kasha and mushroom mixture, cover the saucepan, and place over very low heat. Cook about 12 minutes, until all the liquid has been absorbed and the kasha is tender. Season to taste with salt and pepper. Serve at once or transfer to a casserole dish, cover, and set aside. Shortly before serving, reheat in a 300°F. oven for 10 minutes.

*will do the trick nicely. In this recipe I use less liquid than the usual two-to-one proportion of liquid to grain because the large quantity of onions and mushrooms contributes additional moisture.*

## LIGHTENED CREAMED SPINACH

### Serves 8

1½ pounds fresh spinach, washed and stems removed
2 tablespoons vegetable oil
1 medium onion, chopped
½ cup minced scallions
2 cups low-fat cottage cheese
¼ cup milk
1 teaspoon sugar
1 tablespoon lemon juice
Salt and cayenne pepper to taste

*I have loved creamed spinach, the creamier the better, ever since I was a child. These days, however, few of us consume butter and cream with impunity. Even Julia Child admitted she cut down. Cottage cheese is a suitable low-fat substitute that imparts creaminess with fewer calories.*

Heat the oil in a large skillet. Add the onion and scallions, and sauté until they are tender. Stir in the spinach and cook, stirring, until the liquid in the bottom of the pan has evaporated, about 7 minutes.

Transfer the spinach mixture to a food processor and puree. Return the spinach to the pan. Without washing the food processor, add the cottage cheese and milk and process until smooth. Stir this mixture into the spinach and cook over low heat until any small lumps of cottage cheese have dissolved. Add the remaining ingredients and serve at once or reheat over low heat when ready to serve.

## OLD-FASHIONED POT ROAST

*Serves 8*

2 tablespoons corn oil or unsalted butter
4 pounds boneless beef rump or brisket
2 cups finely chopped onions
1 cup finely chopped celery
1 cup finely chopped carrots
3 garlic cloves, minced
2 cups dry red wine
1½ cups well-flavored beef or veal stock
2 tablespoons tomato paste
Salt and freshly ground black pepper
1½ teaspoons dried thyme
1 bay leaf
2 teaspoons cornstarch dissolved in 2 tablespoons cold water

Preheat the oven to 350°F. Heat the oil in a heavy 4 quart Dutch oven or casserole. Add the beef and brown on all sides over medium-high heat. Remove the meat, lower the heat, and add the onions, celery, and carrots. Cook the vegetables slowly until they are tender and barely beginning to brown. Stir in the garlic.

Return the beef to the casserole. Add the wine, stock, and tomato paste and bring to a simmer. Season to taste with salt and pepper, and add the thyme and bay leaf.

Cover the casserole and place in the oven to bake about 2 hours, or until the meat is tender. If the recipe is being made a day or two in advance, allow the contents of the casserole to cool to room temperature, then refrigerate. Before reheating, remove and discard the layer of fat.

Remove the meat from the casserole. Strain the sauce into a clean saucepan, forcing the vegetables through the sieve. Whisk in the cornstarch mixture. Bring the sauce to a simmer, stirring, until it has thickened slightly. Season again with salt and pepper, if necessary.

Slice the meat and arrange it on a warm platter. Spoon the sauce over the meat and serve.

*S*low-simmered or baked dishes like this are not suited to last-minute preparation and not just because the cooking time is lengthy. To bring out the best flavor and texture it is essential to allow the dish to sit for a day or two after it has been made. That's why I usually reserve this kind of recipe for the weekends, to prepare on Saturday morning perhaps for a Sunday supper.

Today, many cooks select the leanest cuts of rump or brisket to use for pot roast. But more succulent results are obtained if the meat has some fat. For that reason I never buy the first cut of the brisket and sometimes use a boneless shoulder roast. When the pot roast is made in advance the sauce can be chilled and the excess fat skimmed off. The sliced meat can also be reheated in the sauce.

**Tender, succulent pot roast for a weekend dinner**

When I make a pickled fruit or vegetable, a chutney, a relish, or other preserve, I usually do not put up a lifetime supply the way many canning recipes seem to suggest. I fill a few jars, and I do not even bother with exacting canning procedures to make the product shelf-stable. It's easier and more convenient to put my pickles and preserves into jars or containers and store them in the refrigerator, where they keep safely for months.

## CRANBERRY PICKLE

*Makes 3 cups*

1½ cups red wine vinegar
1½ cups sugar
½ cup water
6 thin slices fresh ginger, peeled
½ teaspoon black peppercorns
10 whole cloves
1 cinnamon stick
One 12-ounce package cranberries

Combine the vinegar, sugar, water, ginger, peppercorns, cloves, and cinnamon in a nonreactive saucepan. Bring to a simmer and cook for about 5 minutes, until the sugar has dissolved.

Pick over, rinse, and drain the cranberries; add them to the syrup. Lower heat and cook the berries very slowly, stirring occasionally, until they begin to pop, 5 to 7 minutes. Allow the cranberries to cool in the pan, then transfer to one or more jars or plastic containers and store in the refrigerator. They will keep for a year.

When buying dried fruit try to find the natural kind that has not been treated with sulfur dioxide. The fruit usually is darker and may be less attractive, but that makes no difference for this recipe. I like to use Earl Grey tea, but other teas such as Darjeeling or China black would be fine.

## FRUIT COMPOTE STEEPED IN TEA

*Serves 8*

3 pounds mixed dried fruit
8 cups tea, such as Earl Grey
⅔ cup honey
⅓ cup brandy
2 cinnamon sticks
8 whole cloves

Combine all the ingredients in a heavy saucepan. Simmer very gently for about 35 minutes, until the fruit is tender. You may have to add a little water during the cooking if too much of the liquid evaporates.

Cool to room temperature. Chill before serving.

## Deep Chocolate Chunk Loaf

*Makes 1 large loaf*

6 ounces unsweetened chocolate
1⅓ cups water
1 teaspoon instant coffee
2 cups all-purpose flour
2 teaspoons baking powder
Pinch of salt
½ cup (1 stick) unsalted butter, softened
1¾ cups sugar
3 large eggs
1 teaspoon vanilla extract
1 cup coarsely broken bittersweet chocolate
chunks

Butter a 9 × 5 × 3-inch loaf pan and dust with flour. Preheat the oven to 300°F.

In a saucepan, melt the unsweetened chocolate in the water with the coffee over low heat. Stir until smooth and set aside to cool.

Sift the flour, baking powder, and salt together and set aside.

Cream the butter and sugar in a large bowl. Beat in the eggs one at a time, then stir in the cooled chocolate mixture. Fold in the flour mixture and add the vanilla.

Pour the batter into the prepared pan and bake for 1 hour, 20 minutes, or until a cake tester comes out clean. Remove from the oven, run a knife around the sides of the pan, and unmold the cake onto a rack. Turn the cake upright on a baking sheet. Place the chocolate chunks over the top of the warm cake and return the cake to the oven for about 8 minutes, just until the chocolate softens. Remove the cake from the oven, return it to the rack, and allow to cool.

*This chocolate pound cake, topped with rough-cut chocolate chunks, was inspired by David Liederman, who began using these chunks instead of conventional chips in his cookies in 1979. What goes around comes around. The original Toll House cookies were baked with chunks, not chips.*

*In this recipe the chunks, which baking-chocolate producers have begun to manufacture and sell, give the cake a nice, homey look.*

*A fall holiday spread featuring a roast boneless turkey breast*

# A FALL HOLIDAY MENU

PUMPKIN AND LEEK SOUP
ROAST TURKEY BREAST WITH
SWEET MUSTARD GLAZE
CORN BREAD AND PEPPER DRESSING
SPICED PINEAPPLE CHUTNEY
BRAISED BRUSSELS SPROUTS
CRANBERRY-PECAN PIE
*Leftover Bonus:* TURKEY-LENTIL CASSEROLE

◆

This holiday dinner was created with convenience in mind. All the dishes are straightforward and uncomplicated, and many of them lend themselves to advance preparation and reheating.

Unless the ritual of carving a beautifully burnished turkey at the table figures prominently in your family tradition, this menu would be eminently suited for Thanksgiving or another holiday occasion. Instead of a whole bird, a boned, fresh turkey breast is the centerpiece of this meal, which is especially appropriate if white-meat lovers are in the majority in your family.

The festive array of side dishes, expected at the holiday dinner, guarantees satisfyingly full plates. Seasonal ingredients such as cranberries, pumpkin, and Brussels sprouts are all accounted for. And if your family just says no when Brussels sprouts are served, you can substitute broccoli flowerets cooked for three minutes.

The dressing is baked separately in its own casserole. If your kitchen is equipped with two ovens, preparing this menu presents no problems. But if the turkey, which roasts at 200 degrees, and the dressing, which calls for 375 degrees, cannot be baked in separate ovens, the answer is to prepare the dressing before the turkey, up to the final fifteen minutes of uncovered baking. Then when the turkey has finished roasting and is resting before being carved, the dressing can be returned to the oven for the final stage of baking.

A fruity red wine such as Beaujolais or full-bodied chardonnay are my choices for this menu. At Thanksgiving I especially like to serve one of the newly released Beaujolais nouveaux.

## PUMPKIN AND LEEK SOUP

*Serves 6 to 8*

3 tablespoons unsalted butter
6 leeks, white part only, well rinsed and chopped (about 2 cups)
2 garlic cloves, minced
4½ cups pumpkin in 2-inch cubes
4½ cups water
1½ cups milk or half-and-half
Salt and freshly ground black pepper
1 tablespoon minced fresh chives

Melt the butter in a heavy saucepan. Add the leeks and sauté slowly over low heat until they are tender but not brown, about 10 minutes. Stir in the garlic.

Add the pumpkin and water, cover, and simmer until the pumpkin is tender, about 40 minutes. Allow the mixture to cool for 15 minutes, then puree in one or two batches in a food processor.

Return the puree to the casserole, add the milk or half-and-half, and season to taste with salt and pepper. Reheat before serving. Sprinkle each serving with the chives.

O*ften my first-course choice for a holiday dinner is soup. And with a gathering of immediate family and more distant relatives, it seems easier to find a soup that has universal appeal than some other first-course options.*

*This soup, a velvety, glowing pumpkin puree seasoned with leeks, is a family favorite. Canned or frozen unsweetened pumpkin can be substituted for fresh pumpkin in season, reducing the preparation time considerably.*

## ROAST TURKEY BREAST WITH SWEET MUSTARD GLAZE

*Serves 8*

**1 boneless turkey breast, about 3½ to 4 pounds, rolled and tied**
**½ tablespoon unsalted butter, softened**
**½ tablespoon grainy mustard**
**½ tablespoon light brown sugar**
**Salt and freshly ground black pepper**

*The first time I roasted a whole turkey breast was in the course of testing a recipe by Michel Richard, chef and owner of Citrus restaurant in Los Angeles. His slow-roasting technique produced a sensationally succulent result. Slow cooking does not burnish the outside of the roast, but the mustard glaze enhances its look. Ask your butcher to bone and tie the turkey unless you feel confident you can handle the task yourself.*

Preheat the oven to 200°F. Place the turkey breast on a rack in a roasting pan.

Mix the butter with the mustard and brown sugar, and rub this mixture over the exposed surfaces of the turkey breast. Season lightly with salt and pepper.

Roast the turkey about 3 hours, until a meat thermometer registers 150°F. Remove the turkey from the oven and allow to sit at least 20 minutes before removing the trussing strings and slicing.

## BASIC BUTTERMILK CORN BREAD

*Serves 6 to 8*

**1½ cups yellow cornmeal**
**1 cup all-purpose flour**
**1½ teaspoons baking soda**
**1 teaspoon salt**
**1½ cups buttermilk**
**1 large egg, beaten**
**2 tablespoons corn oil**

*This basic corn bread recipe can also be used to make muffins. Add ¼ cup sugar to the batter.*

Preheat the oven to 400°F. Butter a 9- or 10-inch round baking pan or a cast-iron skillet.

In a large bowl, blend the cornmeal, flour, baking soda, and salt together. Stir in the buttermilk, egg, and oil. Spread the batter in the pan and bake 30 minutes.

## CORN BREAD AND PEPPER DRESSING

*Serves 6 to 8*

2 tablespoons olive oil
1½ cups chopped onions
2 cups chopped red bell pepper
½ cup chopped green bell pepper
½ cup minced scallions
2 tablespoons minced, seeded fresh hot green chilies
5 cups diced, slightly stale Basic Buttermilk Corn Bread (recipe precedes)
⅓ cup chicken stock (approximately)
Salt and freshly ground black pepper

Preheat the oven to 375°F. Grease a 6-cup baking dish attractive enough for serving.

Heat the olive oil in a large skillet. Add the onions and red and green peppers and sauté over medium heat until the vegetables are tender, about 10 minutes. Add the scallions and chilies, and cook over low heat for 10 minutes.

Stir in the corn bread, and add enough stock to moisten the mixture lightly but thoroughly; it should remain a trifle crumbly and not be soaked. Season to taste with salt and pepper. Place in the baking dish and cover with foil. Bake 30 minutes. Uncover and bake 15 minutes longer.

*No turkey is large enough to contain all the stuffing my family will consume, so I always make extra and bake some separately in a casserole.*

*Baking all the stuffing on the side simplifies preparation as well as serving. Gone is the struggle to scrape every last drop out of the turkey while assembled guests wait hungrily for the main course.*

## SPICED PINEAPPLE CHUTNEY

*Makes 4 cups*

1 large pineapple, not too ripe (see note, page 64)
1 cup chopped onion
Juice and grated rind of 2 limes
¼ cup cider vinegar
2 tablespoons dark rum
1 cup light brown sugar, packed
1 teaspoon black peppercorns, crushed
⅛ teaspoon ground cloves

*A relish of some sort is essential on the Thanksgiving table, and a savory chutney fits this bill nicely. Chutneys are Indian in origin and can be made with fruits, vegetables, or both. This chutney is both peppery and sweet. Either can the mixture properly in jars for shelf-stable storage or simply put it into jars or containers and store in the refrigerator, where it will keep for two years—if it isn't all eaten before then!*

Slice the crown of leaves off the pineapple, quarter pineapple lengthwise, then slice out the fibrous core. Peel and dice the quarters.

Place the pineapple in a heavy saucepan and stir in the remaining ingredients. Bring to a boil and cook over medium-high heat for 20 to 25 minutes, until most of the liquid has evaporated and the mixture is thick.

Transfer the hot chutney to sterilized canning jars and seal according to manufacturer's directions, or store in tightly sealed containers in the refrigerator or freezer for up to 2 years.

## BRAISED BRUSSELS SPROUTS

*Serves 8*

2 pints Brussels sprouts
1 medium onion, minced
¼ cup dry white wine
Salt and freshly ground black pepper
2 tablespoons Dijon mustard
⅓ cup heavy cream
1 teaspoon sugar
1 tablespoon white wine vinegar

*Cutting an **X** into the core of each Brussels sprout ensures that it will cook evenly. Take care not to overcook.*

Trim the bottoms of the Brussels sprouts and cut an **X** into the core of each. Place them in a saucepan with the onion and wine, cover tightly, and cook over medium heat about 15 minutes, until the sprouts are just tender. Season them lightly with salt and pepper.

Mix the mustard, cream, sugar, and vinegar in a bowl. Add to the Brussels sprouts and cook for 3 to 4 minutes, until the cream mixture has thickened somewhat. Serve at once.

## PASTRY FOR PIES AND TARTS

*Makes pastry for a 1-crust
8- or 9-inch pie or tart*

1¼ **cups all-purpose flour**
½ **teaspoon salt**
6 **tablespoons (¾ stick) cold unsalted butter,
    diced**
3 **to 4 tablespoons ice water**

To prepare the pastry by hand, mix the flour and salt in a large bowl. Cut in the butter with a pastry blender or your fingertips until the mixture resembles coarse meal. Add the water a tablespoon at a time, tossing the mixture with a fork, until it can be gathered together in a ball. The dough can be used at once but will probably be easier to handle if it is formed into a flat circle, wrapped in plastic, and refrigerated for 30 minutes.

To prepare the pastry in a food processor, place the flour and salt in the container and pulse briefly until combined. Add the butter and pulse briefly, until the butter is about the size of peas. Sprinkle in a little of the water through the feed tube and pulse very briefly. Continue adding water and pulsing until the mixture comes together. Either use immediately or flatten and wrap in plastic, then chill for 30 minutes.

*C*ranberries are native to North America. In colonial days in New England they were called "bounceberries," and they do bounce when dropped. Although they are marketed only in the fall and winter, they are wonderful to keep on hand for making pies, sweet breads, cakes, muffins, and relishes all year. Buy a few extra bags to keep in the freezer; they will last for a year, until the next crop is in the market.

## CRANBERRY-PECAN PIE

*Serves 8*

3½ cups cranberries
⅓ cup coarsely chopped pecans
1 cup plus 3 tablespoons sugar
1½ tablespoons flour
½ cup golden raisins
¼ cup fresh orange juice
½ teaspoon ground cinnamon
3 tablespoons unsalted butter, melted
Pastry for one 9-inch crust (recipe precedes)
1⅓ cups sour cream
½ teaspoon vanilla extract

Preheat the oven to 400°F.

Coarsely chop the berries in a food grinder or food processor. Transfer to a bowl and add the pecans, 1 cup of the sugar, and the flour, raisins, orange juice, cinnamon, and melted butter. Mix thoroughly.

Roll out pastry and place in a 9-inch pie pan. Spoon in the filling. Bake for 45 minutes, until the crust is brown and the filling begins to bubble. Remove from the oven and cool for 30 minutes, leaving the oven on.

Mix the sour cream with the remaining 3 tablespoons of sugar and the vanilla. Spread on top of the pie, return to the oven, and bake 5 minutes to set the topping. Cool completely before serving.

**Cranberry-pecan pie
with sour cream topping**

*In a shift from the fairly stan-dard post-holiday procedure of using leftover turkey in sandwiches or salads, I like to serve a one-dish casserole that combines turkey with lentils and a nice hint of spice. The recipe can also be made into a soup, simply by adding more stock or water.*

*Leftover Bonus:*

# TURKEY-LENTIL CASSEROLE

*Serves 3 to 4*

2 tablespoons extra-virgin olive oil
½ cup chopped onion
½ green bell pepper, seeded and chopped
1 small hot green chili pepper, seeded and chopped
1 cup sliced mushrooms
1 teaspoon minced garlic
1 teaspoon minced fresh ginger
1 teaspoon ground cumin
2 cups chicken or turkey stock or water
1½ cups diced cooked turkey
Salt and freshly ground black pepper
1 cup lentils
⅓ cup dried bread crumbs

Heat 1 tablespoon of the oil in a heavy 2- to 3-quart broiler-proof casserole. Add the onion, green pepper, and chili, and sauté until tender, about 10 minutes. Add the mushrooms and cook, stirring, until they wilt, about 5 minutes. Stir in the garlic and ginger, and continue to cook several minutes longer. Stir in the cumin.

In a separate saucepan, bring the stock or water just to a boil.

Stir the turkey and the hot stock into the sautéed vegetables and season with salt and pepper. Add the lentils. Bring to a boil, cover, and reduce heat. Simmer until the lentils are tender and the liquid has been absorbed, about 45 minutes. Remove from heat.

Preheat the broiler. Uncover the casserole and sprinkle with the bread crumbs. Drizzle on the remaining oil. Place under the broiler just until the top is lightly browned. Serve at once.

# BORSCHT FOR A WINTER WEEKEND

BIG BORSCHT

MUSHROOM PIROSHKI

CUCUMBERS IN MUSTARD DRESSING

IRISH COFFEE TART

◆

This is the perfect supper for a Saturday or Sunday night when there is a crowd of friends or family to entertain. It can be set out buffet style in a dining room, but it's especially inviting when guests can help themselves right in the kitchen. The borscht can be kept warm in a big pot on the stove.

It takes some effort in advance, because the big pot of hearty beef and vegetable borscht must cook for several hours, and actually improves if prepared a day or two in advance. On the other hand, the menu makes relatively few demands on time at the last minute.

It's almost a one-dish meal that needs only a cooling salad of dependably available cucumbers, plus some flaky mushroom-filled turnovers—like Russian piroshki—to round it out. Even these dishes can be made early in the day or the day before, as can the dessert.

The dessert tart boasts a richly mellowed, custardy filling that combines raisins, brown sugar, eggs, and cream with coffee and Irish whiskey.

Nothing but a robust red wine such as zinfandel or Châteauneuf-du-Pape, or a wine such as Cahors or Madiran from the southwestern regions of France will do, unless it's amber beer.

## BIG BORSCHT

*Serves 8*

2 tablespoons vegetable oil
3 pounds beef shanks, with bone, in 1-inch-thick slices
2 medium leeks, mainly the white part, rinsed and chopped
1 red onion, peeled and chopped
2 medium carrots, peeled and chopped
3 garlic cloves, smashed
12 cups water
½ small head red cabbage
¾ pound chopped fresh or drained canned tomatoes
3 sprigs fresh thyme
1 large sprig fresh dill
10 black peppercorns, lightly crushed
2 bay leaves
4 medium beets
4 medium white turnips
2 tablespoons tomato paste
⅓ cup red wine vinegar
Salt
1½ pounds boiling potatoes, peeled
Sour cream or plain yogurt

*This soup-cum-stew makes a hearty meal. I like to cook the potatoes separate from the soup and add them just before serving so they do not become too sodden or discolored. Also, it permits me to freeze leftover soup, because potatoes tend to become mealy when frozen in a home freezer. And this way guests can add the potatoes and sour cream to their borscht to taste. Another way to serve the dish is to place a soup plate with some potatoes before each guest, then ladle the borscht over the potatoes.*

Heat the oil in a large (at least 6-quart) soup pot. Add the beef shanks and brown them on all sides over high heat. Remove the beef and reduce heat to low.

Add the leeks, red onion, and carrots, and sauté until tender but not brown, about 8 minutes. Stir in the garlic. Return the beef to the pot and add 9 cups of the water. Bring to a boil, reduce heat to medium, and cook 5 to 10 minutes, skimming the surface. Reduce heat.

Core and chop the cabbage, and add it to the pot along with the tomatoes. Tie the sprigs of thyme and dill together and add them. Add the peppercorns and bay leaves. Partly cover and simmer for 2 hours.

Scrub the beets and trim off any long bits of root. Cut the stem to within 1 inch of the bulb. Peel the

*Steaming, hearty borscht with potatoes and mushroom piroshki*

turnips. Place the beets and turnips in the pot and continue simmering another hour. By this time the meat should be very tender. If not, simmer up to 1 hour longer.

Remove the meat and the beets and turnips from the pot. Cut the meat off the bones, reserving the marrow, and dice the meat. Return the meat to the pot. Peel the beets and cut into 1-inch chunks. Cut the turnips into chunks. Return both to the pot. Mix the tomato paste with the vinegar and stir it in, along with remaining water. Return soup to a simmer and season to taste with salt. (The soup can now be cooled and refrigerated for up to 3 days.)

Just before serving, cut the potatoes into 1-inch chunks. Boil them in salted water until tender, about 20 minutes, then drain. Place in a warm serving dish. Warm the reserved marrow, dice it, and sprinkle over the potatoes.

Remove the herb sprigs and bay leaves from the borscht. Serve the borscht with the potatoes on the side for guests to add to their soup plates. Serve sour cream or yogurt on the side as well.

## MUSHROOM PIROSHKI

*Makes about 3 dozen*

1 cup all-purpose flour
½ cup (1 stick) cold salted butter
4 ounces cream cheese
6 ounces fresh mushrooms
2 tablespoons extra-virgin olive oil
2 tablespoons finely minced shallots
1 garlic clove, minced
¼ cup heavy cream
1 teaspoon minced fresh thyme, or ½ teaspoon dried
Salt and freshly ground black pepper

*A* basket of these turnovers, still warm, is the perfect savory accompaniment to a hearty bowl of borscht. The pastry is easily prepared and holds up well. The turnovers can be made in advance, baked, and frozen, ready to reheat as needed, so it's convenient to make a double batch and freeze half for later use. I often use other fillings such as the mixtures for the Bruschetti toppings (pages 219 and 222) and serve the turnovers as a hot hors d'oeuvre with drinks.

Place the flour in the bowl of a food processor. Cut the butter into 8 to 10 pieces, add to the food processor, and pulse until the butter is coated with flour and coarsely chopped. Cut the cream cheese into about 8 pieces, add to the food processor, and pulse until a ball of dough can be gathered together.

Pat the dough into a round, wrap in plastic or foil, and refrigerate while preparing the filling.

Quarter the mushrooms, place them in a food processor, and pulse until they are very finely chopped, almost to a paste. Transfer them to a strainer lined with several thicknesses of paper towel and press as much moisture as possible out of the mushrooms.

Heat the oil in a large skillet. Add the shallots and sauté over medium heat until tender and just beginning to color. Stir in the garlic and the mushrooms. Increase the heat to high and sauté, stirring, until the mushrooms are tender and any moisture in the pan has evaporated. Stir in a tablespoon of the cream and season the mixture with thyme, salt, and pepper. The mushroom mixture should be very thick. Set aside to cool.

Roll out the dough on a floured board and cut 3-inch circles. Reroll the scraps and cut more circles. Reroll the scraps and cut as many circles as you can.

Place a scant teaspoon of the mushroom mixture in the center of each circle, pick up the circle, fold it in half over the filling, and press the edges together with your fingertips. Crimp the edge with the tines of a fork. Arrange the filled pastries on one or more baking sheets. The pastries can be frozen at this point and transferred to freezer bags for future use.

Preheat the oven to 400°F. Brush the tops of the pastries with the remaining cream and bake about 25 minutes, until pastry is golden. Serve warm or allow to cool and reheat in the oven for 10 minutes before serving. Frozen pastries can be baked directly from the freezer at 425°F. for 15 to 20 minutes.

## CUCUMBERS IN MUSTARD DRESSING

*Serves 8*

4 medium cucumbers, peeled and seeded
2 tablespoons Dijon mustard
2 tablespoons honey
¼ cup cider vinegar
2 tablespoons extra-virgin olive oil
2 tablespoons minced fresh chives
Freshly ground black pepper to taste

Slice the cucumbers thin and place in a bowl.

Beat the mustard, honey, and vinegar together. Beat in the oil. Pour over the cucumbers and add the chives and pepper. Mix. Serve at once or allow to marinate several hours or overnight.

*Refreshing cucumber salads are simple to prepare, and they can be assembled and dressed in advance with no danger of becoming wilted and soggy as a green salad would. Look for slender cucumbers, which are sweeter, and have smaller seeds, and proportionately more flesh. In summer buy cucumbers that have not been waxed.*

*I*rish coffee, the blend of hot coffee, brown sugar, and Irish whiskey, capped with heavy cream, is said to have been created as an eye-opener for air passengers stopping over at Shannon airport on early transatlantic flights. The same ingredients make a silky, sophisticated pie filling. If you do not have Irish whiskey on hand, scotch, bourbon, or even brandy can take its place. The technique of fully baking the pastry, then filling and rebaking it keeps it very crisp and, magically, it does not become overbaked.

## IRISH COFFEE TART

*Serves 8*

**Pastry for a 9-inch pie (page 167)**
⅓ **cup Irish whiskey**
2 **teaspoons instant coffee**
¼ **cup (½ stick) unsalted butter**
1 **cup raisins**
1 **cup dark brown sugar, packed**
3 **large eggs, beaten**
¾ **cup heavy cream, whipped**

Preheat the oven to 350°F. Roll out the pastry and fit into an 8- or a 9-inch straight-sided tart pan with a removable bottom. Lightly prick the pastry. Fit foil over the pastry and cover it with pastry weights or dried beans. Place in the oven and bake for 10 minutes, until the pastry begins to look dry. Remove the foil and weights and continue baking about 20 minutes longer, until the shell is fully baked.

Heat the whiskey with the coffee in a saucepan until the coffee dissolves. Stir in the butter. When it has melted remove pan from heat and add the raisins and brown sugar, stirring until the brown sugar has dissolved. Beat in the eggs and pour the mixture into the tart shell. Return it to the oven and bake 30 to 35 minutes longer, until it is puffed on top and feels firm to the touch. Allow the tart to cool, then chill. Spread the tart with the whipped cream before serving.

# ROBERT'S MEXICAN-STYLE PARTY SUPPER

ROBERT'S CHILI-BEEF SALAD
GRILLED JALAPEÑO POLENTA
MEXICAN CHOCOLATE SLICES
HONEYDEW-POMEGRANATE SALSA

◆

My son, Robert Fabricant, is an accomplished and inventive cook. He has a particular flair for grilling and for creating vegetable, grain, and bean dishes, as well as a sure hand with seasonings. He is also undaunted, willing to plunge in and bake a pizza with no prior bread-baking experience or try his hand at Indian recipes that call for grinding and mixing whole spices.

The menu he contributed to this collection has a Mexican emphasis. The main-course salad is similar to a fajita without the tortilla wrapper, while the cornmeal polenta seasoned with jalapeño is much more reminiscent of a Southwestern corn bread than of its Italian inspiration. Even the cookies with their touch of cinnamon have the flavors of Mexico.

Only the grilling of the polenta requires last-minute preparation. However, the steak and the beans do call for overnight marinating and soaking. Since the salad is best if the steak is still warm, undercook the meat slightly and keep it wrapped in foil before slicing and adding it to the other ingredients. This dish is suitable for informal buffet entertaining or a family supper.

Robert suggests that beer, preferably an amber beer served with wedges of lime, accompany this menu.

*R*obert wanted to devise a recipe that combined his love for grilling with his passion for beans, vegetables, and salsa. This is the felicitous result. While the salad could be made with canned kidney beans, Robert insists on using dried beans; he even prefers the texture of beans that have been soaked overnight to those that have been parboiled and soaked for an hour. "You have to marinate the meat overnight, so why not soak the beans?" he asks with irrefutable logic. Either way, though, the salad is delicious.

## ROBERT'S CHILI-BEEF SALAD

*Serves 8*

3 large garlic cloves, chopped
½ small onion, diced
¼ cup chili powder
  Salt
¼ cup extra-virgin olive oil
5 tablespoons fresh lime juice
1 pound flank steak
½ pound dried kidney beans
4 large ripe tomatoes
1 medium red onion
1 small red bell pepper, cored and seeded
½ fresh jalapeño pepper, minced
1 ripe Haas avocado
2 tablespoons chopped fresh coriander

Combine the garlic, onion, 2 tablespoons of the chili powder, and ½ teaspoon salt in a blender or food processor. Add 2 tablespoons of the olive oil and 1 tablespoon of the lime juice and process until smooth, then stir in 1 more tablespoon of the chili powder. Rub this mixture into the flank steak. Cover and marinate in the refrigerator overnight.

Soak the beans overnight in water to cover by 2 inches.

Drain the beans and cover with fresh cold water in a large saucepan, to a depth of 1 inch. Bring to a boil, lower the heat, and simmer gently about 45 minutes, until they are tender. Drain and rinse.

Dice the tomatoes, red onion, and bell pepper and place in a large salad bowl. Fold in the jalapeño pepper.

Peel, pit, and dice the avocado and mix it with the remaining 4 tablespoons lime juice, then add them to the bowl. Fold in the beans, the coriander, and the remaining tablespoon of olive oil.

Light a grill or broiler. When it is hot, grill the flank steak about 4 minutes on each side for medium-rare.

Transfer the steak to a cutting board and slice it very thin against the grain at a sharp angle. Cut the slices in half lengthwise, then cut with the grain into pieces about ½ inch wide. Add the meat to the salad, toss lightly, season with salt, and serve.

## GRILLED JALAPEÑO POLENTA

### Serves 8

2 tablespoons corn oil
⅔ cup chopped onion
1 fresh jalapeño pepper, seeded and finely chopped
4 cups water
2 teaspoons salt
1¼ cups yellow cornmeal
⅓ cup shredded cheddar or Monterey Jack cheese
2 tablespoons unsalted butter, melted

*The inspiration for adding jalapeño peppers to polenta came from Robert's sister, Patty. Robert added an extra dimension to this satisfying and refined cornmeal dish by cooking it on the grill.*

Heat the oil in a large, heavy saucepan. Add the onion and the jalapeño and cook over medium heat for about 6 minutes, until tender but not brown. Stir in the water and salt, and bring to a simmer.

With the water simmering, gradually add the cornmeal in a thin stream, stirring constantly. When all the cornmeal has been added, continue to cook the mixture until it is quite thick, about 20 minutes. Remove it from the heat and fold in the cheese.

Butter an 8-inch square baking dish and spread the cooked cornmeal mixture evenly into the dish. Allow it to cool at least 30 minutes.

Light a grill or broiler. Cut the cooled polenta into 8 equal portions and brush each on both sides with melted butter. Grill or broil the polenta until heated through and lightly seared, about 5 minutes on each side.

*Robert's chili-beef salad with*
*grilled jalapeño polenta*

Robert recalled eating cookies such as these when our family visited Oaxaca, Mexico, several years ago. They made a strong impression because they were at once rich and fragrant, yet not as cloying as most of the cakes and pastries sold in Oaxaca's bakeries. Indefatigable testing over a period of several weeks resulted in this recipe for shortbread-style Mexican cookies perfumed with cinnamon. Don't worry if they seem too soft at first; they will firm up as they cool on the baking sheets.

## MEXICAN CHOCOLATE SLICES

*Makes about 40 cookies*

6 ounces unsweetened chocolate
½ cup (1 stick) unsalted butter
1 cup sugar
½ teaspoon salt
½ teaspoon vanilla extract
½ teaspoon ground cinnamon
2 large eggs
2 cups all-purpose flour

Preheat the oven to 375°F.

Place the chocolate and butter in a 2-quart saucepan and melt over very low heat, about 8 minutes. Remove from heat and stir in the sugar, salt, vanilla, and cinnamon. Beat in the eggs one at a time.

Gradually stir in as much flour as you can with a wooden spoon, then transfer the batter to a large bowl or a pastry board and knead in the remaining flour. Divide the dough in half and shape into 2 logs, each about 2 inches in diameter. Cut into slices ½ inch thick and place on baking sheets about an inch apart.

Bake the cookies for 8 minutes. Allow them to cool on the cookie sheets for 15 minutes, then transfer them to cooling racks. They will be very soft when they are first removed from the oven but will crisp as they cool.

## HONEYDEW-POMEGRANATE SALSA

*Serves 8*

**1 large pomegranate**
**1 large ripe honeydew melon, 5 to 6 pounds**
**¼ cup fresh lime juice**

With a sharp knife score the skin of the pomegranate in quarters without cutting into the fruit, and carefully peel away as much of the skin as possible. Gently pull the whole seeds off the membrane and collect them in a bowl, gently breaking the fruit in pieces as you go. Try not to break the seeds. You should have 1 to 1¼ cups of seeds.

Quarter the melon, remove the seeds, and cut off the rind. Cut the melon into 2-inch cubes. Place half the cubes in a food processor and pulse to chop the melon fairly fine. You want small chunky pieces, not a puree. Repeat with the remaining melon. Stir in the lime juice.

Refrigerate the melon and pomegranate seeds separately until serving time.

Spoon the melon into goblets and scatter about a tablespoon of pomegranate seeds over each serving.

*The idea of preparing a slushy dessert with honeydew melon as its base—a dessert "salsa"—was intriguing to both Robert and me. Once the melon was finely chopped and splashed with a little fresh lime juice, it was evident it needed some color.*

*A run through the produce department of the local supermarket yielded a pomegranate, eminently suited for a Mexican menu. If pomegranates are not in season, use cherries.*

# PATTY'S COUSCOUS FEAST

LEAF LETTUCE SALAD WITH
TAHINI-GARLIC DRESSING
PATTY'S VEGETABLE COUSCOUS
HARISSA SAUCE WITH SUN-DRIED TOMATOES
RASPBERRY AND PISTACHIO BREAD PUDDING

◆

Having two children who enjoy sharing meal preparation has been a particular pleasure for me. My daughter, Patty, began cooking in earnest when she moved into her own apartment, and her first attempts were often from my recipes. Now she experiments with confidence, consulting cookbooks for guidance but not for the final preparation.

Her couscous is representative of this evolution. The recipe is rooted in the North African tradition but adapted and seasoned to taste, and made with the vegetables she likes best instead of those that are expected. The fiery harissa sauce was a fortuitous development that came about when she added sun-dried tomatoes to stretch the recipe. Both dishes are perfect for a colorful buffet.

Both the first-course salad and the bread pudding have been seasoned with a Middle Eastern flair—the first with tahini, the other with pistachios and honey.

Either beer or a robust red wine are her choices of beverage. A red Côtes-du-Rhône would suit her budget, as would an inexpensive Chianti.

*The steaming hot saffron- and spice-infused couscous*

## LEAF LETTUCE SALAD WITH TAHINI-GARLIC DRESSING

*Serves 12*

3 medium heads red and green leaf lettuce
2 medium cucumbers, peeled and sliced
2 garlic cloves, finely chopped
2 tablespoons tahini (sesame paste)
⅓ cup white wine vinegar
½ cup extra-virgin olive oil
Salt and freshly ground black pepper

*These days there are many varieties of leaf lettuces on the market. Those grown hydroponically are most convenient because they are very clean, and baby leaf lettuces, too, do not require rinsing and drying. All others—red, green, ruffled, or not—should be rinsed well and thoroughly dried before using.*

Rinse and dry the lettuce. Tear the leaves into bite-size pieces and place them in a large salad bowl. Add the cucumbers.

Mix the garlic and tahini in a bowl, then beat in the vinegar until the ingredients are well blended. Beat in the oil. Season to taste with salt and pepper.

Pour the dressing over the lettuce and cucumbers, toss, and serve.

## PATTY'S VEGETABLE COUSCOUS

*Serves 8 to 10*

5 tablespoons extra-virgin olive oil
2 medium onions, sliced
1 green bell pepper, cored, seeded, and chopped
6 garlic cloves, sliced
6 medium carrots, peeled and cut into 1-inch chunks
1 teaspoon ground cumin
1 teaspoon ground coriander
1 teaspoon ground turmeric
¾ teaspoon ground cinnamon
3 medium sweet potatoes, peeled and cut into 2-inch chunks
1 large eggplant, about 1½ pounds, cut into 2-inch chunks
1 large pinch powdered saffron
7 cups hot well-flavored chicken or vegetable stock

*Couscous is a wonderful party dish, and although this recipe serves up to ten, it's easy to double or even triple it for a larger crowd. The rich vegetable stew can be presented on a large platter, topping the bed of fluffy golden grain as the recipe specifies, or the two parts of the dish can be served in separate large bowls.*

*Patty's recipe is a personal interpretation. It retains some of the*

4 medium, ripe tomatoes, cut into 2-inch chunks
1 cup golden raisins
1 lemon
  Salt, cayenne pepper, and freshly ground black
    pepper to taste
2 cups cooked chick-peas
6 small zucchini, cut into 1-inch chunks
2 cups instant couscous
3 tablespoons minced fresh Italian parsley

Heat 4 tablespoons of the oil in a heavy 6-quart casserole. Add the onions and green pepper, and sauté until tender but not brown, about 6 minutes. Add the garlic and sauté briefly, then stir in the carrots. Sauté until the carrots begin to color, about 8 minutes, then stir in the cumin, coriander, turmeric, and cinnamon. Sauté a few seconds, then stir in the sweet potatoes and eggplant.

Dissolve the saffron in 4 cups of the stock and add the stock to the casserole. Add the tomatoes and raisins. Cut the lemon in half, squeeze the juice into the casserole, and then add the rinds. Bring to a simmer, partly cover, and cook until the carrots and potatoes are tender, about 30 minutes. Season to taste with salt, cayenne pepper, and black pepper. There should be enough liquid in the pan for it to reach about halfway up the vegetables. If not, add a little more water or stock. Stir in the chick-peas and zucchini, bring to a simmer again, remove from heat, and set aside.

While the vegetables are cooking, bring the remaining 3 cups of stock and 1 tablespoon of olive oil to a simmer. Add the couscous, stir briefly, cover, and set aside until the liquid has been absorbed, about 5 minutes. (If the couscous is made in advance, it can be reheated by steaming in a colander lined with cheesecloth.)

To serve, spread the couscous on a large platter. Briefly reheat the vegetable mixture if necessary, then spoon it along with the cooking liquid over the couscous.

Sprinkle with parsley and serve with harissa sauce (recipe follows) on the side.

*classic Moroccan seasonings such as cinnamon, along with ingredients like raisins, eggplant, and chick-peas. But it calls for more tomatoes than might be used traditionally, and it is seasoned to her taste. When I prepare it I sometimes add pieces of turnip, and, occasionally, I have made the vegetable stew using just baby vegetables for an especially handsome party presentation. (But avoid baby eggplants because they are very bitter.)*

*Patty sometimes serves grilled chicken on the side, and she advises that chicken can also be stewed with the vegetables. As you can see, there are many possible variations so don't hesitate to try your own.*

*Patty's vegetable couscous with sun-dried tomato harissa*

## HARISSA SAUCE WITH SUN-DRIED TOMATOES

*In this spicy North African condiment, the sun-dried tomatoes, while unusual, add richness and intensity. They also deepen the color of the sauce.*

*Makes 1 cup*

    2 garlic cloves
    5 red serrano chilies, stems removed
    8 sun-dried tomatoes in oil, drained
 1½ red bell peppers
    6 tablespoons extra-virgin olive oil
 1½ teaspoons hot red pepper flakes, or more to
        taste
    Salt

Finely chop the garlic, chilies, and sun-dried tomatoes by hand or in a mini-food processor.

Hold the red bell pepper over an open flame with tongs or a fork and allow it to char completely. Place in a plastic bag to steam, then rub under running water to remove the skin. Dice the pepper and puree in a food processor along with the minced garlic, chilies, and sun-dried tomatoes.

With the machine running, add the olive oil through the feed tube. Season to taste with pepper flakes and salt. The sauce should be very hot but not inedible.

188

## RASPBERRY AND PISTACHIO BREAD PUDDING

*Serves 12*

**7 cups French bread pieces, torn in 1-inch chunks**
**3½ cups milk**
**¾ cup honey**
**½ teaspoon ground cinnamon**
**4 large eggs, lightly beaten**
**2 cups fresh raspberries**
**¾ cup chopped, blanched, unsalted pistachio nuts**
**2 tablespoons sugar**
**1½ cups heavy cream, softly whipped**

*Honey and pistachios are ubiquitous in Middle Eastern desserts such as baklava. Adding them to a bread pudding makes a delightful hybrid.*

Butter a 2-quart baking dish. Preheat the oven to 350°F.

Place the bread pieces in a large mixing bowl. Heat the milk and honey together in a small saucepan just until the honey dissolves. Add the cinnamon. Pour the milk mixture over the bread and allow it to sit for about 30 minutes, until the bread becomes saturated. Stir in the eggs and fold in the raspberries.

Transfer the mixture to the baking dish. Mix the pistachio nuts and sugar in a bowl and sprinkle over the top. Place dish in the oven and bake about 40 minutes, or until lightly browned on top. Allow the pudding to cool until it is pleasantly warm, then serve with whipped cream.

# A Spicy, Colorful Buffet for Twelve

Sizzled Shrimp
Spicy Jamaican-Style Chicken
Quinoa Salad with Basil
Grilled Ratatouille
Chocolate Banana Cake

◆

I f your guests like spice, this is a menu for them. From the shrimp zapped with garlic and hot peppers served from a sizzling casserole to a homemade version of vibrant Caribbean "jerk" chicken, it keeps the culinary thermostat turned up.

The menu, including the chicken, the ratatouille, the quinoa, and the cake, is convenient to assemble in advance, up to the actual cooking of the shrimp, a job that takes mere minutes. The chicken must be marinated overnight. Although the ratatouille calls for the vegetables to be grilled, they can also be broiled in the oven. The effect will be similar even if the slightly smokey flavor is less evident.

The menu is excellent with beer or sangria. Alternatively, a fruity and full-bodied white wine such as an Australian chardonnay, or a light red, a Beaujolais perhaps, would be suitable.

## SIZZLED SHRIMP

*Serves 12*

2½ **pounds large shrimp (about 50), peeled and deveined**
½ **cup extra-virgin olive oil**
6 **garlic cloves, sliced**
½ **teaspoon hot red pepper flakes**
**Salt to taste**

Rinse the shrimp and pat dry.

Heat the oil in a large, heavy, shallow heatproof casserole, one that can be used over direct heat but is also attractive enough to use for serving and can hold the shrimp in nearly a single layer. If you do not have such a pan, use any sauté pan that is large enough and place an attractive, shallow baking dish in the oven to keep warm.

Add the garlic cloves to the oil, sauté until they just begin to brown, then skim them out and reserve. Stir in the pepper flakes.

Stir in the shrimp and cook over medium-high heat for about 2 minutes, just until the shrimp are cooked through. Remove from the heat and scatter the reserved garlic over the shrimp. Season to taste with salt. Place a toothpick in each shrimp and serve.

*This dish is simply one of the most popular tapas, or hors d'oeuvre, served in Spain. It is easy to prepare in quantity if you have a large skillet or even a paella pan. I like to serve the shrimp, each skewered with a toothpick, from a glazed terra-cotta casserole.*

*Shrimp are graded by size, according to how many there are to a pound. Large shrimp are preferable for this recipe because they can begin to color before becoming overcooked, but are not so large as to make for an awkward mouthful.*

*Appetite-whetting sizzled
shrimp with garlic*

## SPICY JAMAICAN-STYLE CHICKEN

*Traditional Jamaican "jerk" chicken is slow cooked over smoldering allspice wood (called* pimento *in Jamaica) after having been infused with a peppery marinade. The result is more spicy than smokey. This version is not as hotly seasoned (although you can adjust the quantity of red pepper flakes to taste). Nor is it served with the typical, dense Jamaican white bread called* hardough.

*Serves 12*

2 roasting chickens, 4½ to 5 pounds each
4 medium onions
3 garlic cloves
6 scallions
1½ cups soy sauce
2 tablespoons whole allspice, crushed in a mortar
2 tablespoons crushed hot red pepper flakes, or to taste
1 teaspoon grated nutmeg, preferably fresh
2 tablespoons corn oil
1 tablespoon sugar

Split the chickens and place in a large dish.

Coarsely chop the onions, garlic, and 3 of the scallions. Place in a blender or food processor along with the soy sauce and process until it becomes a thick sauce. It should have some texture. Stir in the crushed allspice, pepper flakes, nutmeg, oil, and sugar. Pour this mixture over the chicken, turning to coat the chicken on all sides. Cover and marinate in the refrigerator overnight.

Preheat the broiler.

Drain the chicken, reserving any marinade, and grill or broil *very slowly,* at some distance from the coals or source of heat, about 1½ hours, basting frequently with the marinade. When the chicken is an even, dark brown and the juices run clear when the thigh is pricked, remove it from the broiler and allow to cool for 30 minutes. Heat the remaining marinade to a simmer and baste it again.

When the chicken has cooled, chop it with a cleaver into chunks across the bones. Chop the remaining scallions and sprinkle over the chicken before serving. Serve at room temperature or reheat, covered, in a 250°F. oven, for 30 minutes, then serve.

## QUINOA SALAD WITH BASIL

*Serves 12*

1½ cups quinoa, about ¾ pound, well rinsed
3 cups cold water
2 tablespoons sesame seeds
¼ cup fresh lime juice
⅓ cup cold-pressed sesame oil
1½ tablespoons oriental sesame oil
Salt and freshly ground black pepper
1 cup peeled, seeded, and chopped cucumber
½ cup chopped fresh scallions
⅓ cup chopped fresh basil leaves

Place the quinoa in a large, heavy saucepan with the water. Bring to a boil, cover, lower heat, and simmer gently, about 20 minutes until the water is absorbed and the quinoa is tender. When done, the quinoa will be slightly translucent and each grain will have a tiny ivory-colored ring or "halo" around it.

While the quinoa is cooking, lightly toast the sesame seeds in a dry skillet, under the broiler or in the oven.

Combine the cooked quinoa with the lime juice and oils. Season to taste with salt and pepper. Refrigerate until ready to serve. Fluff it with a fork and adjust seasonings if necessary. Fold in the cucumber, scallions, and basil and transfer to a serving dish. Sprinkle with the toasted sesame seeds.

*Quinoa fascinates me. Pronounced KEEN-wah, it is the seed of a sturdy plant that is best grown at high altitudes, over 10,000 feet. The seed is used as a grain, and is a staple in the diet of Peruvian Indians in the high Andes. It is now cultivated in the Colorado Rockies as well.*

*Containing all ten amino acids and high in calcium, quinoa provides complete protein; in fact, its nutritional profile is similar to that of milk. It has a mild flavor, slightly reminiscent of zucchini or spaghetti squash, and can be used in both savory and sweet dishes.*

*Don't add salt to the cooking water or the grain will become tough.*

## GRILLED RATATOUILLE

### Serves 12

1 large or 2 medium eggplant, about 2 pounds total
2 green bell peppers
2½ pounds zucchini
3 large onions
3 pounds ripe plum tomatoes
¾ cup extra-virgin olive oil (approximately)
5 garlic cloves, minced
Leaves stripped from 3 large sprigs fresh thyme
Salt and freshly ground black pepper
¼ cup finely chopped fresh parsley

*The popularity of grilling has had an impact on ratatouille, the popular French Provençal vegetable mélange. Instead of being sautéed it is now being grilled by chefs across the country. I have been making grilled ratatouille for several years. The pleasantly smokey edge that grilling provides enhances the dish.*

Preheat the grill. Lightly oil a grilling rack.

Slice the eggplant into rounds about ½ inch thick. Core and seed the green peppers and cut them into quarters lengthwise. Slice the ends off the zucchini and cut each in half lengthwise. Peel the onions and slice ½ inch thick. Cut the tomatoes in half lengthwise. Lightly brush the vegetables with some of the olive oil.

Grill the sliced vegetables until nicely seared, turning once to cook both sides. Allow the vegetables to cool briefly, then chop them coarsely into 1-inch pieces.

Heat 4 tablespoons of the olive oil in a large skillet. Add 3 of the garlic cloves, stir for a few seconds, then add the grilled vegetables and thyme. Cook over medium-high heat for 15 to 20 minutes, stirring, until the vegetables soften somewhat but still retain their character. Add the remaining garlic and season to taste with salt and pepper. Stir in the remaining olive oil (about 3 tablespoons). Serve hot, at room temperature, or cold, sprinkled with parsley.

## CHOCOLATE BANANA CAKE

*Serves 12*

¾ cup (1½ sticks) plus 3 tablespoons unsalted
   butter, softened
1½ cups sugar
 3 large eggs
2¼ cups all-purpose flour
1½ teaspoons baking soda
 ¾ teaspoon baking powder
 ½ teaspoon salt
1½ cups pureed ripe banana (about 4 bananas)
1½ teaspoons vanilla extract
 5 ounces semisweet chocolate
 ¼ cup milk
 2 tablespoons dark rum
 1 cup coarsely chopped walnuts
 2 pints ice cream (vanilla, banana, chocolate, rum
   raisin, walnut, or coconut sorbet), optional

Preheat the oven to 350°F. Butter and flour a 9 × 13 × 2-inch oblong baking pan.

In a large mixing bowl, cream ¾ cup butter and the sugar together until light and fluffy. Add the eggs one at a time, beating well after each addition. Sift the flour, baking soda, baking powder, and salt together, then add to the butter mixture alternating with the banana puree. Stir to blend all the ingredients, then add the vanilla.

Spread the batter in the baking pan and bake for about 40 minutes, until the cake is nicely browned and springs back to the touch. Cool completely, then remove from the pan.

In a double boiler, melt the chocolate over hot water, stir in the 3 tablespoons of butter, and cool to room temperature. When cool, beat until smooth. Stir in the milk and rum, beating until the mixture reaches spreading consistency.

Spread the icing on the top of the cooled cake and sprinkle with the walnuts. Cut into squares and serve. If desired, ice cream can be served on the side.

*This moist sheet cake flavored with banana and iced with bittersweet chocolate is an irresistible indulgence for guests and a more interesting use for those overripe bananas than the usual banana bread. Soft bananas are best, so allow several days for yours to ripen, and be sure the walnuts you use taste fresh. Toasting them lightly will improve their flavor.*

*Ice cream is excellent on the side. For a buffet such as this, the most effective way to serve ice cream is to scoop it into a well-chilled 2-quart bowl in advance of the party, then return it to the freezer. At serving time position the bowl in a comfortably larger one filled with ice.*

# A HEARTY BUFFET FOR TWELVE

GINGERED HUMMUS WITH PITA TOASTS
CONFETTI COUSCOUS SALAD
HERB-RUBBED PORK CHOPS
TOMATOES STUFFED WITH SWISS CHARD
HONEY CHEESECAKE WITH PINE NUT CRUST

◆

Because pork chops are wonderful cooked on the grill, this menu is especially suitable for summer entertaining. It could apply to other seasons as well, with the chops oven-broiled or even pan-broiled. There is a very subtle suggestion of the Middle East in the combination of hummus and pita, couscous, and a dessert made with pine nuts and honey, even though pork is definitely not a meat of the Middle East. Lamb chops could be substituted.

Begin the preparation with the hummus and the cheesecake. Like these, the couscous and tomatoes can also be readied early in the day, perhaps while the cheesecake bakes. Give the chops their herb rub and grill them slightly ahead of time so they will be just warm when served. A foil wrapping will keep them that way for a couple of hours.

An agreeable and moderately priced cabernet sauvignon from California, a lesser Bordeaux, or a Côtes-du-Rhône suit the menu beautifully.

## GINGERED HUMMUS WITH PITA TOASTS

### Serves 12

2 garlic cloves
2-inch-long piece of fresh ginger, peeled and chopped
Juice of 4 lemons
2 cups cooked chick-peas
⅔ cup tahini (sesame paste)
Salt
1 tablespoon oriental sesame oil
One 8-ounce package small pita breads

With the machine running, drop the garlic and ginger into a food processor through the feed tube to mince them fine. Turn off the machine and scrape the sides. Add the lemon juice. Turn the machine on again and gradually add the chick-peas, processing until the mixture is pureed. Gradually add the tahini. If the mixture is too thick, add a little water. Season to taste with salt.

Transfer the mixture to a serving bowl and drizzle the sesame oil on top. Cover until ready to serve.

Split the pita breads and cut each round into 4 wedges. Toast the wedges under a broiler or in a toaster oven. Allow to cool and crisp. Serve the hummus with the pita breads for dipping.

*Adding fresh ginger to the already garlicky mixture of sesame paste, lemon, and pureed chick-peas adds a new dimension to this wonderful Middle Eastern dip or spread. Including a splash of nutty brown toasted oriental sesame oil intensifies the flavor. I was amazed at how much ginger was necessary in order for its flavor to emerge in the mixture.*

*Grilled herbed pork chops with confetti couscous*

## CONFETTI COUSCOUS SALAD

An abundance of sweet peppers in a rainbow of colors gives this grain salad its visual panache. Colorful sweet peppers are now sold all year. But in summer when they are locally grown, prices are the most reasonable.

When seeding and coring peppers be sure to remove the fleshy interior ribs.

*Serves 12*

7 tablespoons extra-virgin olive oil
2 medium onions, finely chopped
1 green bell pepper, seeded, cored, and diced
1 red bell pepper, seeded, cored, and diced
1 orange bell pepper, seeded, cored, and diced
1 yellow bell pepper, seeded, cored, and diced
1 tablespoon balsamic vinegar
1½ cups instant couscous
2 cups boiling chicken stock
3 tablespoons minced fresh parsley
Salt and cayenne pepper to taste

Heat 2 tablespoons of the oil in a large skillet. Sauté the onions and peppers until tender. Season with the balsamic vinegar.

Place the couscous in a large bowl. Pour the boiling stock and 4 tablespoons of the olive oil over it, cover, and allow to sit for 5 to 10 minutes, until all the liquid is absorbed.

Fold the pepper mixture, parsley, and additional tablespoon of olive oil into the couscous. Adjust the seasonings. Serve while still warm or allow to cool to room temperature. Fluff with a fork before serving.

## HERB-RUBBED PORK CHOPS

*Serves 12*

24 center-cut pork chops, ½ inch thick (or loin lamb chops)
8 bay leaves
24 sprigs fresh thyme
Salt and freshly ground black pepper
4 lemons, quartered

Trim any excess fat from the edges of the chops and pound the chops lightly. Crumble the bay leaves, chop the thyme, and combine in a small bowl. Rub the chops on both sides with the herbs, place on a platter, cover with foil, and allow to stand at room temperature for 1 hour.

Preheat the barbecue grill. Grill the chops over very hot coals until nicely browned, about 15 minutes for pork chops, 8 minutes for lamb chops. Turn them once during the grilling and move them around if necessary to prevent excess blackening.

Arrange the chops on a serving platter and season with salt and pepper. Arrange the lemon wedges around the chops and serve hot or at room temperature.

*Because these thin pork chops are grilled until they are almost crispy there is no need to worry about whether they have been cooked enough, and the herb rub still comes through. You might consider making a few extra chops; I have known guests to consume three of them in one sitting. If the recipe is prepared using thin lamb chops, it becomes typical of the cooking of the Rioja region of Spain.*

## TOMATOES STUFFED WITH SWISS CHARD

*This is the kind of dish— easy to serve and eat, colorful and appealing at room temperature—that is perfect for a buffet. Be sure all the tomatoes are approximately the same size. As for the Swiss chard, this leafy green vegetable generally is available all year. I love it because it retains its color and crunch even when cooked, but if you can't find any, use spinach.*

*Serves 12*

1 **pound Swiss chard**
12 **medium, ripe tomatoes**
3 **tablespoons extra-virgin olive oil**
3 **garlic cloves, sliced**
¼ **cup chopped scallions**
¼ **cup freshly grated Gruyère cheese**
**Salt and freshly ground black pepper**

Rinse the chard, drain, and chop it fine.

Slice the tops off the tomatoes about ½ inch down and reserve. Scoop out the pulp, leaving tomato shells. Chop the pulp and place it in a strainer suspended over a bowl to drain. Discard the liquid.

Heat the oil in a large skillet. Add the garlic, sauté for a minute or so, then add the chopped chard. Cook, stirring, until the chard begins to wilt, 2 to 3 minutes, then cover the pan and cook over low heat for 15 minutes. Uncover the pan and add the tomato pulp and scallions. Cook, stirring, a few minutes longer.

Fold in the cheese and season with salt and pepper. Remove from heat and allow to cool briefly.

Fill the tomato shells evenly with the chard mixture. Replace the tops of the tomatoes if you wish. Arrange the tomatoes on a platter.

## HONEY CHEESECAKE WITH PINE NUT CRUST

*Serves 12*

1¾ cups pine nuts
3 tablespoons dry bread crumbs
¼ cup sugar
1 pound cream cheese, softened
3 large eggs
⅓ cup plus 2 tablespoons honey
1½ tablespoons grated orange rind
1 teaspoon vanilla extract

Preheat the oven to 375°F. Reserve 1 tablespoon of the pine nuts and place the remaining nuts in a food processor with the bread crumbs and sugar. Process until the nuts are finely ground and begin to cling together but still have some texture; you do not want a nut butter.

Press the nut mixture evenly into the bottom and at least 1 inch up the sides of a 10-inch springform cake pan. Place in the oven and bake 6 to 8 minutes, until the crust begins to color and smell toasty. Remove the pan from the oven and lower the oven temperature to 325°F.

Place the cream cheese in the food processor (you needn't clean it) along with the eggs, ⅓ cup of the honey, orange rind, and vanilla. Process until smooth. Pour this mixture into the nut crust, place in the oven, and bake about 45 minutes, just until the cake is firm to the touch.

Allow the cake to cool completely, then refrigerate it until chilled. Toast the tablespoon of reserved pine nuts by tossing them in a dry skillet over medium heat for 3 to 4 minutes. Spread the remaining 2 tablespoons of honey over the top of the cake. Decorate it with the toasted pine nuts.

*A lush and velvety cheesecake is one of the supreme indulgences. No wonder it remains such a popular dessert.*

*This one is enriched with honey and baked in a crust made with ground pine nuts for a different, almost Middle Eastern cast. The inspiration for the pine nut crust comes from Thomas Keller, an exceedingly talented chef, who fills it with a lemon sabayon for a combination that is even richer than the cheesecake, if that is possible.*

*Think of the pastry for other uses—for a simple fruit tart or even with a chocolate filling.*

*Because this dessert is very rich I find the recipe ample for 12 servings even though it has been baked in a 10-inch pan.*

# A BRUNCH BUFFET FOR TWELVE

MELON MARGARITAS

BLACK BEAN CAKES WITH SMOKED SALMON

OVERNIGHT FRENCH TOAST WITH
SUMMER FRUIT CONSERVE

RADICCHIO, RED ONION, AND
RASPBERRY SALAD

PUMPKIN-NUT LOAF WITH
FROMAGE BLANC

◆

This colorful menu remains rooted in the breakfast tradition, with smoked salmon and French toast; and with the exception of the French toast, this menu would please the fitness minded.

The day before the buffet, prepare the fromage blanc, the pumpkin-nut loaf, and the preliminaries for the French toast and black bean cakes, leaving only the frying of the French toast and the black bean cakes at the last minute. The fruit conserve can be put up weeks in advance, of course, but they can also be prepared the day before. The salad should be made in the morning. Although the fromage blanc and pumpkin-nut loaf are oriented toward dessert, they should be put on the buffet along with the rest of the food.

Along with the margaritas, it's important to serve coffee and tea. Fresh orange juice, with or without Champagne, is suitable, too.

*Creamy overnight French toast and bracing melon margaritas*

## MELON MARGARITAS

*Serves 12 to 16*

2 medium honeydew melons, chilled
Juice of 12 limes
2 cups tequila
½ cup fresh orange juice
1 cup Cointreau or triple sec

*Adding pureed honeydew melon to margaritas intensifies the green color and fresh flavor while diminishing the alcoholic impact of the drink.*

Peel and seed the melons and cut them into cubes. Puree the melon cubes in a food processor. Mix the melon puree with the remaining ingredients. Stir with ice in a pitcher or pour into glasses over ice.

## BLACK BEAN CAKES WITH SMOKED SALMON

*Serves 12*

3 cups cooked black beans
3 large eggs, beaten
¾ cup whole wheat flour
Salt and cayenne pepper to taste
4 tablespoons corn oil
¾ cup sour cream or plain yogurt
8 ounces smoked salmon, cut in thin strips
2 tablespoons minced fresh chives

*The mashed black beans in this batter make the small pancakes resemble blini. These are stunning with their topping of sour cream and smoked salmon, but salmon caviar would also be attractive and tasty. Keep them in mind as cocktail hors d'oeuvre for dinner parties; they are delicious with a glass of Champagne.*

Mash the beans and place them in a food processor. Add the eggs and process to blend. Transfer to a bowl, mix in the flour, and season to taste with salt and pepper.

Preheat the oven to 150°F.

Heat the oil in one or more heavy skillets. Drop tablespoons of batter into the skillet, flattening each portion into a round cake about 3 inches in diameter. Fry on both sides, then transfer to a platter. Place the fried cakes in the oven to keep warm while you make the rest.

Top each cake with a dollop of sour cream or yogurt, a few strips of the salmon, and a sprinkling of chives.

## OVERNIGHT FRENCH TOAST

*Serves 12 to 16*

1 pound Egg Bread (page 210), firm white bread, or brioche loaf
12 large eggs
1 tablespoon vanilla extract
3 tablespoons granulated sugar
2 tablespoons grated orange peel
½ teaspoon freshly grated nutmeg
1¼ cups half-and-half
½ cup (1 stick) unsalted butter
Confectioners' sugar

Slice the bread into 1-inch-thick slices and spread them in a single layer in 1 or 2 baking pans. If the slices are large, halve or quarter them.

Beat the eggs until well blended but not frothy. Add the vanilla extract, granulated sugar, grated orange peel, and nutmeg, then stir in the half-and-half. Pour this over the bread, turn the slices to coat both sides, cover, and refrigerate overnight.

Preheat the oven to 150°F.

Melt some of the butter in 1 or 2 heavy skillets over medium heat and fry the bread slices, turning them once, until lightly browned on both sides. Add more butter as needed. Transfer the cooked slices to a baking sheet and place in the oven to keep warm.

Just before serving, dust the toast with sifted confectioners' sugar.

*I can remember, as a student in France, being stunned to discover that French toast was indeed French. There it is called* pain perdu, *or "lost bread," and it is served as a dessert. Of course the authentic recipe calls for the leftover stale baguette that can inevitably be found in a French kitchen. Here it is made with a richer bread such as challah or brioche. Allowing the bread to soak overnight gives the French toast an inviting, custardy texture. Serve it with a dollop of the fruit conserve.*

*A brunch buffet ready to serve*

## SUMMER FRUIT CONSERVE

*Makes 3 cups*

2 pounds plums, preferably both red and purple
3 medium peaches
Juice and grated rind of 1 orange
½ cup light brown sugar, packed
3 tablespoons honey
2 teaspoons ground cardamom

Peel, pit, and chop the plums. Place them in a large, heavy saucepan and begin to heat them very slowly.

Peel, pit, and chop the peaches and add half to the saucepan. Puree the rest of the peaches in a blender or food processor until smooth, add the puree to the saucepan along with the remaining ingredients.

Cook slowly over low heat for about 40 minutes, stirring occasionally, until the mixture is thick but some of the fruit still holds its shape. Taste and adjust the sweetness.

*As* with the other jams and preserves in this book, I prefer to prepare small batches of this conserve and store a container or two of it in the refrigerator without bothering with sterilizing and sealing standard canning jars. A mixture of red and purple plums is prettiest.

## RADICCHIO, RED ONION, AND RASPBERRY SALAD

*Serves 12*

3 medium heads radicchio
1 medium red onion, peeled and sliced paper thin
1 cup fresh raspberries
⅓ cup raspberry vinegar
⅓ cup extra-virgin olive oil
Salt and freshly ground black pepper

Remove the cores from the radicchio and separate the heads into leaves, breaking any large leaves into smaller pieces. Place in a salad bowl. Add the onion and all but 3 tablespoons of the raspberries.

Mash the reserved raspberries into the vinegar. Beat in the olive oil. Season to taste with salt and pepper. Pour the dressing over the salad. The salad can be served immediately, but it is better if it marinates for 1 hour.

*Radicchio, small heads of deep burgundy leaves streaked with white, belong to the endive family. They are colorful, crunchy, and pleasantly bitter. Ten years ago Americans were hardly aware that radicchio existed. Now it's grown here as well as imported from Italy, and available in supermarkets. A leafier variety, tinged with green as well as maroon, is called Treviso.*

## EGG BREAD

*A* wonderfully rich loaf, almost a brioche, this is the bread I prefer for my Tomato Sandwiches (page 214) and Cheese Toasts (page 150).

*Makes 2 loaves*

2 packages active dry yeast
Pinch of sugar
¼ cup warm water (105°–115°F.)
3 large eggs
2 tablespoons honey
2 teaspoons salt
1 cup milk, scalded and cooled to tepid
6 cups all-purpose flour (approximately)
1 egg yolk beaten with 1 teaspoon cold water

Dissolve the yeast and sugar in the warm water and set aside to proof for 5 minutes.

Meanwhile, beat the eggs until they begin to thicken. Beat in the honey, salt, and milk. Add the yeast mixture. Slowly beat in 2½ cups of the flour. Then beat in another 2½ cups flour, ½ cup at a time, until the dough cleans the sides of the mixing bowl. (This step can be done by hand or machine.)

Turn out onto a floured board and knead for 10 minutes, kneading in another ½ to 1 cup flour. The dough should be smooth, elastic, and supple. Place the dough in a well-oiled bowl, turn to oil all sides, cover, and set aside in a warm place to rise until doubled, about 1 hour.

Punch dough down and divide in half. Butter two 8½ × 4½ × 2-inch loaf pans. Pat each piece of dough into a flat rectangle. Roll tightly, jelly-roll fashion, and pinch the ends closed. Place each roll of dough seam side down in one of the prepared pans. Cover and allow to rise until the dough has doubled and risen to the tops of the pans, about 45 minutes. Brush the tops with beaten egg yolk.

Preheat the oven to 350°F.

Bake the bread for about 40 minutes, until nicely browned. Cool the loaves briefly, then turn out onto cooling racks and cool completely before slicing.

## PUMPKIN-NUT LOAF

*Makes 1 large loaf*

- ½ cup (1 stick) unsalted butter, softened
- ⅔ cup granulated sugar
- ⅓ cup light brown sugar, packed
- 2 large eggs
- 1 cup whole wheat flour
- 1 cup all-purpose flour
- 2 teaspoons baking powder
- ¼ teaspoon baking soda
- ½ teaspoon salt
- ½ teaspoon ground cinnamon
- ¼ teaspoon ground cloves
- 1 cup unseasoned pumpkin puree, fresh, frozen, or canned
- 1½ cups chopped mixed nuts (pecans, walnuts, hazelnuts, etc.)

*R*ich and moist, this fragrant, nut-studded quick bread can be served with breakfast, brunch, as a tea cake, or even with a traditional Thanksgiving dinner. Use whatever nuts you like—a mixture is excellent—but be sure they are fresh. Lightly toasting the nuts improves their flavor. Serve the bread plain or with Fromage Blanc (page 47).

Preheat the oven to 350°F. Butter and flour a 9 × 5 × 3 inch loaf pan.

Cream together the butter and sugars, then beat in the eggs one at a time.

Sift the flours with the baking powder, baking soda, salt, and spices. Stir dry mixture into the batter, alternating with the pumpkin puree. Stir in the chopped nuts.

Spread the batter in the prepared pan and bake about 1 hour, 10 minutes, or until a cake tester comes out clean. Cool 20 minutes in the pan, then turn out onto a rack and continue cooling before slicing.

# A SUMMER BUFFET FOR TWELVE

TOMATO SANDWICHES

SAVORY ONION PUDDING WITH CORN

BARBECUED TUNA

ROMAINE LETTUCE WITH
GORGONZOLA DRESSING

CHOCOLATE AND FRUIT IN PHYLLO

◆

This summertime spread that takes advantage of seasonal produce begins with simple "tea" sandwiches of tomato and mayonnaise on bread. The tuna is grilled in an old-fashioned red barbecue sauce that enhances its steaklike taste and texture; a savory bread pudding provides a substantial complement. Dessert is an irresistible combination of brandied chocolate and fruit enclosed in a crisp parchmentlike package of phyllo.

The tomato sandwiches, the salad, and the dessert (up to the actual baking) are all suited to advance preparation, but keep the lettuce and the dressing separate until shortly before serving. The tuna can be grilled during the cocktail hour or just before, but be careful not to overcook it. Have the bread pudding prepared and ready to go in the preheated oven the moment the first guest arrives.

A smooth red wine such as a Rioja or a cabernet sauvignon from Chile will complement the food at a modest price. It would not be a mistake to have a full case on hand, to avoid any anxiety of running out of wine.

*Chocolate and fruit wrapped in phyllo*

## TOMATO SANDWICHES

*Serves 12*

**18 thin slices Egg Bread (page 210)**
**½ cup mayonnaise**
**4 to 5 ripe tomatoes, thinly sliced**

*T*his simple hors d'oeuvre has almost become a signature dish for me. A note about buying tomatoes: those that are fully rounded, with no deep indentation at the stem end, will be easier to slice and are less likely to be woody in the center.

Lightly spread the bread with a thin layer of the mayonnaise. Arrange the tomatoes in a single layer on half of the slices. Top each sandwich with a second slice of bread, and cut into 4 triangles.

## SAVORY ONION PUDDING WITH CORN

*Serves 12*

**4 tablespoons (½ stick) unsalted butter**
**1½ cups finely chopped onion**
**4 scallions, minced**
**1 jalapeño pepper, seeded and minced**
 **Kernels stripped from 6 ears fresh corn**
 **Salt and freshly ground black pepper**
**4 large eggs, beaten**
**2 to 2½ cups milk**
**1 loaf stale French bread, about 10 ounces,**
 **thinly sliced**

*W*hy do bread puddings have to be sweet? By incorporating vegetables and omitting the sugar I arrived at this savory bread pudding that is spiked with a little hot pepper. Served warm, it's a lovely addition to a summer buffet.

Preheat the oven to 350°F. Generously butter a shallow 3-quart baking dish or casserole.

Melt 1 tablespoon of butter in a skillet, add the onion, scallions, and jalapeño; sauté until soft but not brown, about 8 minutes. Stir in the corn. Season to taste.

Mix the eggs and milk in a bowl. Add the bread slices and press to saturate them. Line the bottom of the baking dish with some of the bread. Scatter on some of the vegetables and repeat layers, ending with bread. Pour any remaining milk and eggs over the top and dot with remaining butter. Bake for about 1 hour, until lightly browned.

## BARBECUED TUNA

*Serves 12*

**4 pounds tuna steaks, 1¼ inches thick**
**One 6-ounce can tomato paste**
**¾ cup red wine vinegar**
**¼ cup light soy sauce**
**Tabasco or cayenne pepper to taste**

Trim any very dark flesh from the tuna and cut the steaks into 12 uniform pieces. Place them in a large, shallow bowl.

Combine the remaining ingredients and pour over the tuna, turning to coat all sides. Marinate 2 to 3 hours.

Preheat a barbecue grill. Cook the tuna over very hot coals, turning the pieces once, until well-seared on the outside and still rare in the very center, 3 to 5 minutes per side. Baste with the marinade while grilling.

*This is tuna treated like beef-steak, with the application of a thick red barbecue sauce. While I prefer the richness of good beef sizzled on a grill unadorned, tuna can be on the bland side, and is leaner than steak, so it needs some sauce or marinade to encourage it to become crusty on the outside. Other fish steaks—mako, swordfish, salmon—can be substituted.*

## ROMAINE LETTUCE WITH GORGONZOLA DRESSING

*Serves 12*

**2 large heads romaine lettuce**
**½ cup white wine vinegar**
**6 ounces Gorgonzola cheese, mashed**
**¾ cup extra-virgin olive oil**
**Salt and freshly ground black pepper**
**½ cup finely chopped fresh parsley**

Remove the cores from the heads of lettuce, separate the leaves, and rinse and dry them. Tear them into bite-size pieces and place in a large salad bowl.

Mix the vinegar with the cheese, then stir in the oil. Pour over the lettuce and toss. Season to taste with salt and pepper and sprinkle with parsley.

*When including a green salad such as this one on a buffet, tear the pieces of lettuce quite small so the salad can be eaten comfortably and will not monopolize the dinnerplate. If Gorgonzola cheese is unavailable, another variety of blue-veined cheese can be substituted. But the texture should be creamy, not dry.*

## CHOCOLATE AND FRUIT IN PHYLLO

*Serves 12*

**7 ounces bittersweet chocolate, chopped**
**½ cup heavy cream**
**⅓ cup brandy**
**½ cup plus 1 tablespoon sugar**
**⅓ cup boiling water**
**8 sheets phyllo dough**
**½ cup (1 stick) unsalted butter, melted**
   **Quick Chocolate Génoise (recipe follows) or other chocolate cake (see Note)**
**1½ cups fresh fruit (raspberries, diced pitted cherries, peeled and diced pears, or a mixture)**

"This is the best dessert I have ever tasted," my daughter, Patty, said when we were first served it at Le Cirque in New York. One bite and we were all willing to forgo this famous restaurant's celebrated crème brûlée for this latest confection devised by the talented young pastry chef, Jacques Torres.

Into packages of phyllo go a thin layer of chocolate cake topped with a creamy trufflelike ganache mixture, then some fresh fruit. Upon baking, the ganache melts into the chocolate cake, its sweetness balanced by the tartness of the fruit. Although Jacques makes it just with raspberries, I have found that other fruits, even a tutti-frutti mixture, work equally well.

The dessert can be assembled and refrigerated, needing only a final baking before serving, adding to its appeal on a menu for entertaining.

Place the chocolate in a bowl. Heat the cream to boiling in a small saucepan, pour over the chocolate, and set aside until the chocolate melts. Stir to combine the cream and chocolate, then stir in 2 tablespoons of the brandy. Set aside to cool.

Dissolve the ½ cup sugar in the boiling water, add the remaining brandy, and set aside.

Spread 1 sheet of the phyllo dough on a work surface. Brush with some of the melted butter and top with another sheet of phyllo. Brush with butter and sprinkle with a teaspoon or so of sugar. Cut the double thickness of phyllo horizontally into 3 equal strips, each about 5 inches wide.

Using a 2½-inch cookie cutter, cut the cake into 12 equal discs. Place a disc of the chocolate cake in the center of each strip. Brush with some of the reserved brandy syrup and top with a generous spoonful of the chocolate and cream mixture. Top with a tablespoonful or two of the fruit, then fold the ends of the phyllo over the top, tucking them under. Fold the sides down and tuck them under, completely enclosing the chocolate and raspberry assembly as if wrapping a sandwich in wax paper. Repeat with the remaining ingredients, making 12 phyllo packages.

Place the packages on a baking sheet and brush

them with melted butter. Refrigerate until shortly before serving time.

Preheat the oven to 350°F. Bake about 15 minutes, until lightly browned. Cool about 5 minutes, then arrange on a platter and serve.

**N o t e :** Almost any plain chocolate cake cut to a ½-inch thickness can be used. If necessary, plain white cake can be substituted. The following recipe makes just enough cake for this recipe.

## QUICK CHOCOLATE GÉNOISE

*Makes one 8-inch layer*

¼ **cup cocoa, preferably Dutch processed**
½ **cup all-purpose flour**
 3 **large eggs, at room temperature**
¼ **cup sugar**
 2 **tablespoons clarified butter**

Preheat the oven to 350°F. Butter and flour an 8-inch round cake pan.

Sift the cocoa and flour together.

Place the eggs in a bowl of an electric mixer and beat with a hand-held mixer or a whisk over simmering water until they are warm. Beat in the sugar. Remove the bowl from the simmering water and beat with the electric mixer until very light and fluffy, at least 5 minutes.

Fold in the flour mixture, then the clarified butter. Spread the batter in the prepared pan and bake about 20 minutes, until the cake springs back when touched.

Allow the cake to cool in the pan before removing. Split it in half horizontally and cut into discs to use in the above recipe.

*A classic French sponge cake used as a basis for everything from petits fours to lavish, multi-layered confections, génoise is typically made as a plain cake. But it takes to flavorings beautifully, chocolate in this case, but also citrus, liqueur, and nut. The key is gently warming the eggs so they will increase in volume when beaten. Be sure they are at room temperature when you begin the recipe.*

# ITALIAN FLAVORS IN A BUFFET FOR SIXTEEN

BRUSCHETTI WITH CHICKEN LIVER SPREAD
AND PEPPER SPREAD
GARLICKY BEAN SALAD
BUFFET CHICKEN WITH ARUGULA
SUMMER PUDDING

◆

Except for the dessert, this attractive buffet is Italian in its inspiration. The appetizers of toast rounds spread with either a chicken liver paste or a mash of peppers are ubiquitous in Tuscany, as is the bean salad. The chicken is my invention, involving lightly grilled chicken breasts, conveniently kept on hold in a warm oven, then topped with verdant arugula leaves and shavings of Parmesan cheese, a nod to a typical presentation of carpaccio.

The dessert is a British classic and can only be made when an assortment of fresh berries is available. It is stunning and delicious. It requires minimal cooking, a boon in summer; but it must be started very early in the day or, better still, the day before. As with the summer pudding, the bean salad can be made in advance up to a day or two before. The toppings for the bruschetti can be prepared early in the day, but should not be spread on the bread until shortly before serving. The chicken should be marinated and the other ingredients for this dish assembled hours before serving. Grill the chicken before guests arrive, but do not arrange it for serving until dinnertime.

A chardonnay from California, Australia, or the Macon could accompany this menu. For sixteen guests you should have a full case on hand.

# BRUSCHETTI WITH CHICKEN LIVER SPREAD

*Serves 16*

1 **pound fresh chicken livers**
5 **tablespoons extra-virgin olive oil**
3 **garlic cloves, minced**
2 **tablespoons anchovy paste**
  **Salt and freshly ground black pepper**
2 **tablespoons finely minced fresh Italian parsley**
32 **thin slices Italian or French baguette, lightly toasted**

Pick over the chicken livers, removing any discolored spots. Dry livers on paper towels.

Heat 3 tablespoons of the oil in a heavy skillet over medium heat, add the garlic, sauté for a few seconds, then add the chicken livers. Sauté livers, stirring and turning them, until they are just cooked through, about 10 minutes. Do not permit them to become hard.

Puree the chicken livers in a food processor. Season with anchovy paste and work in the remaining 2 tablespoons of oil to give the mixture spreading consistency. Season to taste with salt and pepper and mix in the parsley. Spread evenly on the toast and serve.

Whether they are called bruschetti or crostini, I find that toasted rounds of good country bread topped with a savory mix of some sort has the virtue of being convenient to prepare and serve as well as inviting to eat. These Italian nibbles can be topped with mushrooms, or mashed smoked fish or olives . . . the list is endless.

This bruschetti variation has a rich, pâtélike spread. Note that the chicken liver bruschetti will discolor if prepared in advance unless they are covered with plastic wrap placed directly on the surface.

*A party buffet of bruschetti,*
*chicken with arugula,*
*and garlicky bean salad*

## BRUSCHETTI WITH PEPPER SPREAD

*This version of bruschetti is less rich than the chicken liver variety, so allow three per person rather than two.*

### Serves 16

6 tablespoons extra-virgin olive oil
2 large red bell peppers, cored, seeded, and finely chopped
2 large onions, peeled and finely chopped
3 garlic cloves, minced
3 tablespoons chopped fresh basil
12 sun-dried tomatoes in oil, drained and minced
1 tablespoon anchovy paste
48 thin slices Italian or French baguette, lightly toasted
Basil leaves and olives, for garnish

Heat the oil in a skillet over medium heat. Add the peppers and onions, and sauté until they are tender, about 10 minutes. Stir in the garlic and basil, sauté a moment longer, then remove from heat. Stir in the sun-dried tomatoes. Chop this mixture nearly to a paste or puree it in a food processor. Season with the anchovy paste.

Spread the pepper mixture evenly on the toasted bread and garnish platters with fresh basil leaves and olives.

## GARLICKY BEAN SALAD

*Bean salads are a favorite for buffet entertaining. They are relatively uncomplicated to prepare in quantity, inexpensive, and are stylish. And they are healthful besides.*

*I recommend speckled pinto beans for this recipe, but almost any other variety—navy beans, cannellini, kidney beans, black*

### Serves 16

3 cups dried pinto beans
4 teaspoons finely chopped garlic
½ cup chopped fresh Italian parsley
⅔ cup extra-virgin olive oil
1 teaspoon salt, or to taste
Freshly ground black pepper

Place the beans in a saucepan with water to cover by a depth of 2 inches and soak overnight. Alternatively, place in a saucepan, bring to a boil, and cook for 2 minutes; remove from heat, then soak the beans for 1 hour.

Drain the beans, cover with fresh cold water, bring to a simmer, and cook, partly covered, until tender, about 40 minutes. Drain.

Transfer the beans to a bowl and gently mix with the garlic, parsley, ½ cup of the oil, salt, and pepper. Allow to cool to room temperature, about 30 minutes. Just before serving check the seasonings and drizzle with remaining 2 tablespoons of olive oil.

*beans, or one of the newer types such as Appaloosas—can be used.*

*Canned beans (cannellini or pink beans) may be substituted. You will need about three pounds. Rinse them thoroughly before using.*

## BUFFET CHICKEN WITH ARUGULA

### Serves 16

Juice of 2 lemons
2 large garlic cloves, crushed
⅔ cup extra-virgin olive oil
Freshly ground black pepper
20 skinless and boneless chicken breasts
¼ cup balsamic vinegar
1 tablespoon Dijon mustard
1 bunch arugula, rinsed, dried, and stems removed
¼ pound Parmesan cheese, shaved

*This is an easy and inexpensive way to feed a crowd. The tangy marinated chicken is first seared on a grill or under a broiler, then placed in a slow oven until serving time; it will continue to cook (but not overcook) as it warms. The saladlike topping adds color, a contrasting bitter edge to the flavor, and a textural counterpoint, yet won't become soggy as it sits on the buffet.*

Combine the lemon juice, garlic, 2 tablespoons olive oil, and pepper in a shallow glass dish. Coat the chicken breasts with the marinade, cover, and marinate 2 hours.

About 1½ hours before serving, grill or broil the chicken over high heat, turning each breast once, until lightly browned on the outside but not quite cooked through, about 10 minutes.

Preheat the oven to 150°F. Transfer the chicken to a shallow baking dish, cover, and place in the oven. The chicken can be kept this way for 20 minutes to 1 hour. It will continue to cook. Beat the vinegar and mustard together and beat in the remaining oil. Set aside.

To serve, arrange the chicken on a serving platter. Cover the chicken with the arugula leaves. Drizzle the dressing over the arugula and scatter the cheese on top.

*A spectacular summer pudding filled with mixed berries*

## SUMMER PUDDING

To make this show-stopping dessert, a bowl is closely lined with thin crustless slices of firm-textured white bread, then filled with a sweetened mixture of seasonal berries cooked only long enough to release their juices. More

*Serves 16*

**Two 1-pound loaves thin-sliced white sandwich bread**

3 cups sugar
  **Juice of 2 lemons**

5 pints mixed fresh berries, such as raspberries, strawberries, blueberries, blackberries, fresh currants

⅓ cup framboise (raspberry *eau-de-vie*)

3 cups heavy cream, whipped

Select two 2-quart round mixing bowls. Remove the crusts from the bread and arrange the slices, trimming them to shape where necessary, to completely line both bowls, with no gaps. Reserve the remaining bread for covering the top.

Place the sugar in a heavy 3-quart saucepan over low heat. Stir in the lemon juice. When the sugar starts to melt after a couple of minutes, add the berries. Stir gently and cook until all the sugar has dissolved and the berries have given up their juices, 5 to 8 minutes. The berries should be soft but still hold their shape, and there should be a rich berry-colored syrup in the pan. Add the framboise.

Using a slotted spoon, transfer the berries to the 2 bread-lined bowls. Pour all but about ½ cup of the syrup over the tops. The bowls should be nearly filled. Fit pieces of the reserved bread on top of each pudding to cover the berries.

Place a china plate that will fit into the bowls on top of each pudding. Place a heavy jar or tin can on top to weight the pudding. Some of the syrup will begin to ooze up and that's fine.

Refrigerate the puddings and the reserved syrup at least 8 hours or overnight.

To serve, run a knife around the inside of each bowl and unmold the puddings onto plates with enough of a rim to catch any excess syrup. Use the reserved syrup to paint any areas where the color did not completely soak in. Serve at once, with whipped cream on the side.

*bread is added to cover the bowl, and the assembly is refrigerated and weighted, for a number of hours or overnight. The weighting firms the texture enough to allow the pudding to be unmolded easily. The berry juices seep into the bread, coloring it a deep magenta. All the pudding needs is a drift of unsweetened whipped cream.*

# A SEAFOOD BUFFET FOR TWENTY

DUCK RILLETTES
GRAND AÏOLI
NECTARINES AND BLACKBERRIES
IN BRANDIED BLACKBERRY SAUCE

◆

From a simple but delectable appetizer to the dazzling assortment of ingredients for the grand aïoli, this is a show-stopping menu. By carefully selecting the fish, shellfish, and vegetables for the aïoli, then cooking each separately and arranging them artfully on your platters, you create a splendid array. Guests who prefer to keep calories to a minimum might resist the rich, garlicky sauce on the side.

The duck rillettes require lengthy but unattended cooking and are best prepared a day or two in advance. The dessert is also quite simple and lends itself to early preparation. The aïoli ingredients should be assembled, ready to cook, by late afternoon. Begin by cooking the vegetables, then go on to the fish and seafood. By starting the preparation two to three hours before serving time, the ingredients will have cooled to room temperature but not remain unrefrigerated too long. If you must refrigerate them, be sure to bring them to room temperature.

A crisp white wine such as a sauvignon blanc complements the aïoli. Brut Champagne or sparkling wine would be another excellent choice with the duck rillettes as well as the aïoli. A case and a half should be ample.

## DUCK RILLETTES

*Serves 20 to 24*

1 duck, 4½ to 5 pounds
1 bottle dry white wine
1 teaspoon green peppercorns
4 garlic cloves
  Salt and freshly ground black pepper
  Toast, bread, or unsalted crackers

Remove the breast from the duck, bone and all, leaving any fat or skin, and use in another recipe or freeze for later use. (See the recipe for Duck Lo Mein, page 132.)

Cut up the rest of the duck, place it in a heavy saucepan, and add the wine, peppercorns, and garlic cloves. Bring to a gentle simmer, cover, and cook for about 3 hours, until the duck is very tender, most of the wine has evaporated, and the duck pieces are cooking in clear fat.

Pour the contents of the saucepan into a colander suspended over a large bowl to catch the drippings.

Remove all the skin and bones from the duck and discard. (If you wish, you can save the skin and fry it to make cracklings to add to a salad.)

Shred the duck meat with your fingers, 2 forks, or by briefly pulsing it in a food processor fitted with a plastic blade. Transfer the shredded duck to a bowl and gradually stir in all but ¼ cup of the fat, mixing it to incorporate well. You should now have a mixture the texture of peanut butter but with a certain chewiness. Season it carefully with salt and pepper and transfer the rillettes to one or more crocks. Pour a thin film of the reserved fat over the top.

Refrigerate the rillettes but remove from the refrigerator 30 minutes before serving. Serve with toast, bread, or crackers.

*T*he most basic of pâté mixtures, rillettes amount to little more than meat and fat, mashed together and seasoned. The rich spreadable paste, a staple in many French households, has a delectable succulence. The cooking is slow and lengthy but requires little attention, and if you make extra rillettes, they can be frozen for up to two months.

*Poached seafood and vegetables with garlic mayonnaise make the grand aïoli.*

# GRAND AÏOLI

*Serves 20 to 24*

40 very small new potatoes, peeled (or 10 larger new
   potatoes, quartered)
Salt
 1 head broccoli, trimmed into flowerets
½ head cauliflower, trimmed into flowerets
40 very thin asparagus
40 baby carrots, scraped and with an inch of stem
   left on (or 10 larger carrots, quartered
   lengthwise)
 1 bottle dry white wine
 6 pounds mussels, scrubbed and debearded
48 jumbo shrimp, peeled
 3 pounds salmon fillet with the skin
 2 pounds halibut, cod, or tilefish steaks
 2 large eggs
 4 large garlic cloves
 3 tablespoons white wine vinegar
 2 cups light olive oil
½ teaspoon saffron threads
 2 tablespoons boiling water
   Lemon wedges, Italian parsley, Niçoise olives, and
   quartered hard-cooked eggs, for garnish

This bountiful spread of sea-food and vegetables with garlic mayonnaise (aïoli) is a wonderful party dish. The preparation is somewhat time-consuming because each ingredient must be cooked separately to prevent overcooking. To serve up to two dozen guests, I prefer to arrange all the vegetables on one platter, the fish and seafood on another. There should be a good variety of ingredients but feel free to make substitutions. For example, the vegetable platter could include whole baby zucchini or yellow squash, or lightly steamed inch-thick rounds of larger summer squash. Green or wax beans, poached leeks or small white onions, or baby white turnips are some other possibilities. Do not use baby eggplants because they tend to be bitter. The types of fish can also be varied, but they should be meaty varieties that take well to poaching (blackfish, black cod, hake, monkfish, or skate are a few

Start the preparation 2 to 3 hours in advance. Boil the potatoes in salted water until just tender, 15 to 20 minutes. Drain, place in a bowl, cover, and set aside.

Steam the broccoli and cauliflower until crisp-tender, about 3 minutes. Rinse briefly in cold water, drain and transfer to a bowl, cover, and set aside.

Steam the asparagus until just tender, about 2 minutes. Rinse briefly under cold water, drain, and set aside on a plate, covered.

Steam the carrots until tender, about 10 minutes. Set aside on a plate, covered.

In a very large, shallow pan—about 7-quart capacity—or in 2 pots, bring the wine to a simmer. Add the mussels and cover and steam until they open, about 10 minutes. Remove the mussels in their shells from the pan with a slotted spoon, discarding any that do not open. Transfer them to a bowl and cover.

If the mussel liquid in the pan looks fairly clean, you can continue with the recipe, but if it looks full of silt, strain it through a fine strainer and return it to the pan, or one of the pans if 2 were used. Add the shrimp and cook about 2 minutes, just until they turn pink. Remove the shrimp with a slotted spoon. Place in a bowl and cover.

Cut the salmon into sections only to make it fit into the pan. Poach it gently in the mussel broth until it is just cooked through, 8 to 10 minutes. Remove the salmon, draining it well, then cook the halibut the same way. Place the cooked fish on a plate and cover.

To make the aïoli sauce, place the eggs in a food processor and add the garlic and vinegar. Process until mixed. Add the oil through the feed tube in a slow, thin stream and continue processing until the mixture emulsifies into a mayonnaise. Steep the saffron briefly in the boiling water and add to the mayonnaise. Process to blend. Season the aïoli with salt to taste. If you use commercial mayonnaise, season it with minced garlic and steeped saffron.

To serve, arrange the vegetables, fish, and seafood attractively on one or more large platters. Cut the fish into serving pieces if desired. You can use one platter for the seafood and fish and another for the vegetables. Garnish the fish with lemon wedges and olives; the vegetables with hard-cooked eggs and parsley. Serve with a bowl of the aïoli on the side.

*to try); and among the seafood you might offer chunks of lobster meat, large sea scallops, crab claws, or rings of squid.*

*If you feel uneasy about making mayonnaise with raw eggs because of the risk of salmonella contamination, use commercial mayonnaise and season it with garlic and saffron.*

## NECTARINES AND BLACKBERRIES IN BRANDIED BLACKBERRY SAUCE

*Serves 20 to 24*

**12 to 14 large, ripe nectarines**
**¼ cup lemon juice**
**3 pints fresh blackberries**
**⅓ cup sugar**
**¾ cup blackberry brandy, or ½ cup brandy or Cognac**
**Crème fraîche (optional)**

*A dessert that combines seasonal freshness with attractive color and ease of preparation is to be treasured. Nectarines, because they do not require peeling, are the fruit of choice, and they are beautifully complemented by lush blackberries. Simple cookies like Toasted Coconut Macaroons (page 110) or Mexican Chocolate Slices (page 182) are excellent on the side.*

Slice the nectarines, discarding the pits. Place in a bowl and toss lightly with the lemon juice.

Press half the blackberries through a sieve to remove the seeds and place in a small saucepan. Add the sugar and heat gently just until the sugar has dissolved, 3 to 4 minutes. Stir in the brandy.

Mix the remaining blackberries with the nectarines in a large glass bowl, pour the sauce over the fruit, and toss gently. Refrigerate until ready to serve. If desired, a bowl of crème fraîche can be served on the side.

# INDEX